Fifty Famous People

James Baldwin

Table of Contents

Table of Contents

Fifty Famous People

Fifty Famous People

James Baldwin

Kessinger Publishing reprints thousands of hard–to–find books!

Visit us at http://www.kessinger.net

PREFATORY NOTE

One of the best things to be said of the stories in this volume is that, although they are not biographical, they are about real persons who actually lived and performed their parts in the great drama of the world's history. Some of these persons were more famous than others, yet all have left enduring "footprints on the sands of time" and their names will not cease to be remembered. In each of the stories there is a basis of truth and an ethical lesson which cannot fail to have a wholesome influence; and each possesses elements of interest which, it is believed, will go far towards proving the fallibility of the doctrine that children find delight only in tales of the imaginative and unreal. The fact that there are a few more than fifty famous people mentioned in the volume may be credited to the author's wish to give good measure.

SAVING THE BIRDS

One day in spring four men were riding on horseback along a country road. These men were lawyers, and they were going to the next town to attend court.

There had been a rain, and the ground was very soft. Water was dripping from the trees, and the grass was wet.

The four lawyers rode along, one behind another; for the pathway was narrow, and the mud on each side of it was deep. They rode slowly, and talked and laughed and were very jolly.

As they were passing through a grove of small trees, they heard a great fluttering over their heads and a feeble chirping in the grass by the roadside.

"Stith! stith! stith!" came from the leafy branches above them.

"Cheep! cheep! cheep!" came from the wet grass.

"What is the matter here?" asked the first lawyer, whose name was Speed. "Oh, it's only some old robins!" said the second lawyer, whose name was Hardin. "The storm has blown two of the little ones out of the nest. They are too young to fly, and the mother bird is making a great fuss about it."

"What a pity! They'll die down there in the grass," said the third lawyer, whose name I forget.

"Oh, well! They're nothing but birds," said Mr. Hardin. "Why should we bother?"

"Yes, why should we?" said Mr. Speed.

The three men, as they passed, looked down and saw the little birds fluttering in the cold, wet grass. They saw the mother robin flying about, and crying to her mate.

Then they rode on, talking and laughing as before. In a few minutes they had forgotten about the birds.

But the fourth lawyer, whose name was Abraham Lincoln, stopped. He got down from his horse and very gently took the little ones up in his big warm hands.

They did not seem frightened, but chirped softly, as if they knew they were safe.

"Never mind, my little fellows," said Mr. Lincoln "I will put you in your own cozy little bed."

[Illustration]

Then he looked up to find the nest from which they had fallen. It was high, much higher than he could reach.

But Mr. Lincoln could climb. He had climbed many a tree when he was a boy. He put the birds softly, one by one, into their warm little home. Two other baby birds were there, that had not fallen out. All cuddled down together and were very happy.

Soon the three lawyers who had ridden ahead stopped at a spring to give their horses water.

"Where is Lincoln?" asked one.

All were surprised to find that he was not with them.

"Do you remember those birds?" said Mr. Speed. "Very likely he has stopped to take care of them."

In a few minutes Mr. Lincoln joined them. His shoes were covered with mud; he had torn his coat on the thorny tree.

"Hello, Abraham!" said Mr. Hardin. "Where have you been?"

"I stopped a minute to give those birds to their mother," he answered.

"Well, we always thought you were a hero," said Mr. Speed. "Now we know it."

Then all three of them laughed heartily. They thought it so foolish that a strong man should take so much trouble just for some worthless young birds.

"Gentlemen," said Mr. Lincoln, "I could not have slept to—night, if I had left those helpless little robins to perish in the wet grass."

Abraham Lincoln afterwards became very famous as a lawyer and statesman. He was elected president. Next to Washington he was the greatest American.

ANOTHER BIRD STORY

A great battle had begun. Cannon were booming, some far away, some near at hand. Soldiers were marching through the fields. Men on horseback were riding in haste toward the front.

"Whiz!" A cannon ball struck the ground quite near to a company of soldiers. But they marched straight onward. The drums were beating, the fifes were playing.

"Whiz!" Another cannon ball flew through the air and struck a tree near by. A brave general was riding across the field. One ball after another came whizzing near him.

"General, you are in danger here," said an officer who was riding with him. "You had better fall back to a place of safety."

[Illustration]

But the general rode on.

Suddenly he stopped at the foot of a tree. "Halt!" he cried to the men who were with him. He leaped from his horse. He stooped and picked up a bird's nest that had fallen upon the ground. In the nest were some tiny, half—fledged birds. Their mouths were open for the food they were expecting their mother to give them.

"I cannot think of leaving these little things here to be trampled upon," said the general.

He lifted the nest gently and put it in a safe place in the forks of the tree.

"Whiz!" Another cannon ball.

4

He leaped into the saddle, and away he dashed with his officers close behind him.

"Whiz! whiz! whiz!"

He had done one good deed. He would do many more before the war was over. "Boom! boom! boom!"

The cannon were roaring, the balls were flying, the battle was raging. But amid all the turmoil and danger, the little birds chirped happily in the safe shelter where the great general, Robert E. Lee, had placed them. "He prayeth best, who loveth best All things both great and small; For the dear God who loveth us, He made and loveth all."

SPEAKING A PIECE

Two children, brother and sister, were on their way to school. Both were very small. The boy was only four years old, and the girl was not yet six. "Come, Edward, we must hurry," said the sister. "We must not be late." With one hand the little boy clung to his sister's arm, and with the other he held his primer.

This primer was his only book, and he loved it. It had a bright blue cover, which he was careful not to soil. And in it were some odd little pictures, which he never grew tired of looking at.

Edward could spell nearly all the words in his primer, and he could read quite well.

The school was more than a mile from their home, and the children trotted along as fast as their short legs could carry them.

At a place where two roads crossed, they saw a tall gentleman coming to meet them. He was dressed in black, and had a very pleasant face.

"Oh, Edward, there is Mr. Harris!" whispered the little girl. "Don't forget your manners."

They were glad to see Mr. Harris, for he was the minister. They stopped by the side of the road and made their manners. Edward bowed very gracefully, and his sister curtsied.

"Good morning, children!" said the minister; and he kindly shook hands with both.

[Illustration]

"I have something here for little Edward," he said. Then he took from his pocket a sheet of paper on which some verses were written.

"See! It is a little speech that I have written for him. The teacher will soon ask him to speak a piece at school, and I am sure that he can learn this easily and speak it well"

Edward took the paper and thanked the kind minister.

"Mother will help him learn it," said his sister.

"Yes, I will try to learn it," said Edward.

"Do so, my child," said the Minister; "and I hope that when you grow up you will become a wise man and a great orator."

Then the two children hurried on to school.

The speech was not hard to learn, and Edward soon knew every word of it. When the time came for him to speak, his mother and the minister were both there to hear him.

He spoke so well that everybody was pleased. He pronounced every word plainly, as though he were talking to his schoolmates.

Would you like to read his speech? Here it is:—

> Pray, how shall I, a little lad,
> In speaking make a figure?
> You're only joking, I'm afraid—
> Just wait till I am bigger.
>
> But since you wish to hear my part,
> And urge me to begin it,
> I'll strive for praise with all my heart,
> Though small the hope to win it.
>
> I'll tell a tale how Farmer John
> A little roan colt bred, sir,
> Which every night and every morn
> He watered and he fed, sir.
>
> Said Neighbor Joe to Farmer John,
> "You surely are a dolt, sir,
> To spend such time and care upon
> A little useless colt, sir."
>
> Said Farmer John to Neighbor Joe,
> "I bring my little roan up
> Not for the good he now can do,
> But will do when he's grown up."
>
> The moral you can plainly see,

To keep the tale from spoiling,
The little colt you think is me—
I know it by your smiling.

And now, my friends, please to excuse
My lisping and my stammers;
I, for this once, have done my best,
And so—I'll make my manners.

The little boy's name was Edward Everett. He grew up to become a famous man and one of our greatest orators.

WRITING A COMPOSITION

"Children, to–morrow I shall expect all of you to write compositions," said the teacher of Love Lane School. "Then, on Friday those who have done the best may stand up and read their compositions to the school."

Some of the children were pleased, and some were not.

"What shall we write about?" they asked.

"You may choose any subject that you like best," said the teacher.

Some of them thought that "Home" was a good subject. Others liked "School." One little boy chose "The Horse." A little girl said she would write about "Summer."

The next day, every pupil except one had written a composition.

"Henry Longfellow," said the teacher, "why have you not written?"

"Because I don't know how," answered Henry. He was only a child.

"Well," said the teacher, "you can write words, can you not?"

"Yes, sir," said the boy.

"After you have written three or four words, you can put them together, can you not?"

"Yes, sir; I think so."

"Well, then," said the teacher, "you may take your slate and go out behind the schoolhouse for half an hour. Think of something to write about, and write the word on your slate. Then try to tell what it is, what it is like, what it is good for, and what is done with it. That is the way to write a composition."

Henry took his slate and went out. Just behind the schoolhouse was Mr. Finney's barn. Quite close to the barn was a garden. And in the garden, Henry saw a turnip.

"Well, I know what that is," he said to himself; and he wrote the word *turnip* on his slate. Then he tried to tell what it was like, what it was good for, and what was done with it.

Before the half hour was ended he had written a very neat composition on his slate. He then went into the house, and waited while the teacher read it.

The teacher was surprised and pleased. He said, "Henry Longfellow, you have done very well. Today you may stand up before the school and read what you have written about the turnip."

Many years after that, some funny little verses about Mr. Finney's turnip were printed in a newspaper. Some people said that they were what Henry Longfellow wrote on his slate that day at school.

But this was not true. Henry's composition was not in verse. As soon as it was read to the school, he rubbed it off the slate, and it was forgotten. Perhaps you would like to read those funny verses. Here they are; but you must never, *never*, NEVER think that Henry Longfellow wrote them.

>Mr. Finney had a turnip,
>And it grew, and it grew;
>It grew behind the barn,
>And the turnip did no harm.
>
>And it grew, and it grew,
>Till it could grow no taller;
>Then Mr. Finney took it up,
>And put it in the cellar.
>
>There it lay, there it lay,
>Till it began to rot;
>Then Susie Finney washed it
>And put it in a pot.
>
>She boiled it, and boiled it,
>As long as she was able;
>Then Mrs. Finney took it,
>And put it on the table.
>
>Mr. Finney and his wife
>Both sat down to sup;
>And they ate, and they ate,
>They ate the turnip up.

All the school children in our country have heard of Henry W. Longfellow. He was the best loved of all our poets. He wrote "The Village Blacksmith," "The Children's Hour," and many other beautiful pieces which you will like to read and remember.

THE WHISTLE

Two hundred years ago there lived in Boston a little boy whose name was Benjamin Franklin.

On the day that he was seven years old, his mother gave him a few pennies.

He looked at the bright, yellow pieces and said, "What shall I do with these coppers, mother?"

It was the first money that he had ever had.

"You may buy something, if you wish," said his mother.

"And then will you give me more?" he asked.

His mother shook her head and said: "No, Benjamin. I cannot give you any more. So you must be careful not to spend these foolishly."

The little fellow ran into the street. He heard the pennies jingle in his pocket. How rich he was!

Boston is now a great city, but at that time it was only a little town. There were not many stores.

As Benjamin ran down the street, he wondered what he should buy. Should he buy candy? He hardly knew how it tasted. Should he buy a pretty toy? If he had been the only child in the family, things might have been different. But there were fourteen boys and girls older than he, and two little sisters who were younger.

What a big family it was! And the father was a poor man. No wonder the lad had never owned a toy.

He had not gone far when he met a larger boy, who was blowing a whistle.

"I wish I had that whistle," he said.

The big boy looked at him and blew it again. Oh, what a pretty sound it made!

"I have some pennies," said Benjamin. He held them in his hand, and showed them to the boy. "You may have them, if you will give me the whistle." "All of them?"

"Yes, all of them."

"Well, it's a bargain," said the boy; and he gave the whistle to Benjamin, and took the pennies.

Little Benjamin Franklin was very happy; for he was only seven years old. He ran home as fast as he could, blowing the whistle as he ran.

"See, mother," he said, "I have bought a whistle."

"How much did you pay for it?"

"All the pennies you gave me."

"Oh, Benjamin!"

One of his brothers asked to see the whistle.

"Well, well!" he said. "You've paid a dear price for this thing. It's only a penny whistle, and a poor one at that."

"You might have bought half a dozen such whistles with the money I gave you," said his mother.

The little boy saw what a mistake he had made. The whistle did not please him any more. He threw it upon the floor and began to cry.

"Never mind, my child," said his mother, very kindly. "You are only a very little boy, and you will learn a great deal as you grow bigger. The lesson you have learned to–day is never to pay too dear for a whistle." Benjamin Franklin lived to be a very old man, but he never forgot that lesson.

Every boy and girl should remember the name of Benjamin Franklin. He was a great thinker and a great doer, and with Washington he helped to make our country free. His life was such that no man could ever say, "Ben Franklin has wronged me."

THE ETTRICK SHEPHERD

I

In Scotland there once lived a poor shepherd whose name was James Hogg. His father and grandfather and great–grandfather had all been shepherds.

It was his business to take care of the sheep which belonged to a rich landholder by the Ettrick Water. Sometimes he had several hundreds of lambs to look after. He drove these to the pastures on the hills and watched them day after day while they fed on the short green grass.

He had a dog which he called Sirrah. This dog helped him watch the sheep. He would drive them from place to place as his master wished. Sometimes he would take care of the whole flock while the shepherd was resting or eating his dinner.

One dark night James Hogg was on the hilltop with a flock of seven hundred lambs. Sirrah was with him. Suddenly a storm came up. There was thunder and lightning; the wind blew hard; the rain poured.

The poor lambs were frightened. The shepherd and his dog could not keep them together. Some of them ran towards the east, some towards the west, and some towards the south.

The shepherd soon lost sight of them in the darkness. With his lighted lantern in his hand, he went up and down the rough hills calling for his lambs.

Two or three other shepherds joined him in the search. All night long they sought for the lambs.

Morning came and still they sought. They looked, as they thought, in every place where the lambs might have taken shelter.

At last James Hogg said, "It's of no use; all we can do is to go home and tell the master that we have lost his whole flock."

They had walked a mile or two towards home, when they came to the edge of a narrow and deep ravine. They looked down, and at the bottom they saw some lambs huddled together among the rocks. And there was Sirrah standing guard over them and looking all around for help "These must be the lambs that rushed off towards the south," said James Hogg.

[Illustration]

The men hurried down and soon saw that the flock was a large one.

"I really believe they are all here," said one.

They counted them and were surprised to find that not one lamb of the great flock of seven hundred was missing.

How had Sirrah managed to get the three scattered divisions together? How had he managed to drive all the frightened little animals into this place of safety?

Nobody could answer these questions. But there was no shepherd in Scotland that could have done better than Sirrah did that night.

Long afterward James Hogg said, "I never felt so grateful to any creature below the sun as I did to Sirrah that morning."

II

When James Hogg was a boy, his parents were too poor to send him to school. By some means, however, he learned to read; and after that he loved nothing so much as a good book.

There were no libraries near him, and it was hard for him to get books. But he was anxious to learn. Whenever he could buy or borrow a volume of prose or verse he carried it with him until he had read it through. While watching his flocks, he spent much of his time in reading. He loved poetry and soon began to write poems of his own. These poems were read and admired by many people.

The name of James Hogg became known all over Scotland. He was often called the Ettrick Shepherd, because he was the keeper of sheep near the Ettrick Water.

Many of his poems are still read and loved by children as well as by grown up men and women. Here is one:—

A BOY'S SONG

Where the pools are bright and deep,
Where the gray trout lies asleep,
Up the river and o'er the lea,
That's the way for Billy and me.

Where the blackbird sings the latest,
Where the hawthorn blooms the sweetest,
Where the nestlings chirp and flee,
That's the way for Billy and me.

Where the mowers mow the cleanest,
Where the hay lies thick and greenest,
There to trace the homeward bee,
That's the way for Billy and me.

Where the hazel bank is steepest,
Where the shadow falls the deepest,
Where the clustering nuts fall free,
That's the way for Billy and me.

Why the boys should drive away,
Little maidens from their play,
Or love to banter and fight so well,
That's the thing I never could tell.

But this I know, I love to play
In the meadow, among the hay—
Up the water, and o'er the lea,
That's the way for Billy and me.

THE CALIPH AND THE POET

Once upon a time there was a famous Arab [Footnote: Ar'ab.] whose name was Al Mansur. He was the ruler of all the Arabs, and was therefore called the caliph. [Footnote: Caliph (*pronounced* ka'lif).]

Al Mansur loved poetry and was fond of hearing poets repeat their own verses. Sometimes, if a poem was very pleasing, he gave the poet a prize. One day a poet whose name was Thalibi [Footnote: Thal i'bi.] came to the caliph and recited a long poem. When he had finished, he bowed, and waited, hoping that he would be rewarded.

"Which would you rather have" asked the caliph, "three hundred pieces of gold, or three wise sayings from my lips?"

The poet wished very much to please the caliph. So he said, "Oh, my master, everybody should choose wisdom rather than wealth."

The caliph smiled, and said, "Very well, then, listen to my first wise saying: When your coat is worn out, don't sew on a new patch; it will look ugly."

"Oh, dear!" moaned the poet. "There go a hundred gold pieces all at once." The caliph smiled again. Then he said, "Listen now to my second word of wisdom. It is this: When you oil your beard, don't oil it too much, lest it soil your clothing."

"Worse and worse!" groaned the poor poet. "There go the second hundred. What shall I do?"

"Wait, and I will tell you," said the caliph; and he smiled again. "My third wise saying is—"

"O caliph, have mercy!" cried the poet. "Keep the third piece of wisdom for your own use, and let me have the gold."

The caliph laughed outright, and so did every one that heard him. Then he ordered his treasurer to pay the poet five hundred pieces of gold; for, indeed, the poem which he had recited was wonderfully fine.

The caliph, Al Mansur, lived nearly twelve hundred years ago. He was the builder of a famous and beautiful city called Bagdad.

"BECOS! BECOS! BECOS!"

Thousands of years ago the greatest country, in the world was Egypt.

It was a beautiful land lying on both sides of the wonderful river Nile. In it were many great cities; and from one end of it to the other there were broad fields of grain and fine pastures for sheep and cattle.

Fifty Famous People

The people of Egypt were very proud; for they believed that they were the first and oldest of all nations.

"It was in our country that the first men and women lived," they said. "All the people of the world were once Egyptians."

A king of Egypt, whose name was Psammeticus, [Footnote: Psammeticus (*pro.* sam met'i kus).] wished to make sure whether this was true or not. How could he find out?

He tried first one plan and then another; but none of them proved anything at all. Then he called his wisest men together and asked them, "Is it really true that the first people in the world were Egyptians?"

They answered, "We cannot tell you, O King; for none of our histories go back so far."

Then Psammeticus tried still another plan.

He sent out among the poor people of the city and found two little babies who had never heard a word spoken. He gave these to a shepherd and ordered him to bring them up among his sheep, far from the homes of men. "You must never speak a word to them," said the king; "and you must not permit any person to speak in their hearing."

The shepherd did as he was bidden. He took the children far away to a green valley where his flocks were feeding. There he cared for them with love and kindness; but no word did he speak in their hearing.

They grew up healthy and strong. They played with the lambs in the field and saw no human being but the shepherd.

Thus two or three years went by. Then, one evening when the shepherd came home from a visit to the city, he was delighted to see the children running out to meet him. They held up their hands, as though asking for something, and cried out, "Becos! becos! becos!"

[Illustration]

The shepherd led them gently back to the hut and gave them their usual supper of bread and milk. He said nothing to them, but wondered where they had heard the strange word "becos," and what was its meaning.

After that, whenever the children were hungry, they cried out, "Becos! becos! becos!" till the shepherd gave them something to eat.

Some time later, the shepherd went to the city and told the king that the children had learned to speak one word, but how or from whom, he did not know.

"What is that word?" asked the king.

"Becos."

Then the king called one of the wisest scholars in Egypt and asked him what the word meant.

"Becos," said the wise man, "is a Phrygian [Footnote: Phrygian (*pro.* frij'i an).] word, and it means *bread.*"

"Then what shall we understand by these children being able to speak a Phrygian word which they have never heard from other lips?" asked the king.

"We are to understand that the Phrygian language was the first of all languages," was the answer. "These children are learning it just as the first people who lived on the earth learned it in the beginning."

"Therefore," said the king, "must we conclude that the Phrygians were the first and oldest of all the nations?"

"Certainly," answered the wise man.

And from that time the Egyptians always spoke of the Phrygians as being of an older race than themselves.

This was an odd way of proving something, for, as every one can readily see, it proved nothing.

A LESSON IN HUMILITY

One day the caliph, Haroun–al–Raschid, [Footnote: Haroun–al–Raschid (*pro.* ha roon' al rash'id).] made a great feast. The feast was held in the grandest room of the palace. The walls and ceiling glittered with gold and precious gems. The table was decorated with rare and beautiful plants and flowers.

All the noblest men of Persia [Footnote: Per'sia.] and Arabia [Footnote: A ra'bi a.] were there. Many wise men and poets and musicians had also been invited.

In the midst of the feast the caliph called upon the poet, Abul Atayah, [Footnote: A'bul Ata'yah.] and said, "O prince of verse makers, show us thy skill. Describe in verse this glad and glorious feast."

The poet rose and began: "Live, O caliph and enjoy thyself in the shelter of thy lofty palace."

"That is a good beginning," said Raschid. "Let us hear the rest." The poet went on: "May each morning bring thee some new joy. May each evening see that all thy wishes have been performed."

"Good! good!" said the caliph, "Go on."

The poet bowed his head and obeyed: "But when the hour of death comes, O my caliph, then alas! thou wilt learn that all thy delights were but a shadow."

[Illustration]

The caliph's eyes were filled with tears. Emotion choked him. He covered his face and wept.

Then one of the officers, who was sitting near the poet, cried out: "Stop! The caliph wished you to amuse him with pleasant thoughts, and you have filled his mind with melancholy."

"Let the poet alone," said Raschid. "He has seen me in my blindness, and is trying to open my eyes."

Haroun–al–Raschid (Aaron the Just) was the greatest of all the caliphs of Bagdad. In a wonderful book, called "The Arabian Nights," there are many interesting stories about him.

THE MIDNIGHT RIDE

> Listen, my children, and you shall hear
> Of the midnight ride of Paul Revere.
> Longfellow.

The midnight ride of Paul Revere happened a long time ago when this country was ruled by the king of England.

There were thousands of English soldiers in Boston. The king had sent them there to make the people obey his unjust laws. These soldiers guarded the streets of the town; they would not let any one go out or come in without their leave.

The people did not like this. They said, "We have a right to be free men, but the king treats us as slaves. He makes us pay taxes and gives us nothing in return. He sends soldiers among us to take away our liberty."

The whole country was stirred up. Brave men left their homes and hurried toward Boston.

They said, "We do not wish to fight against the king, but we are free men, and he must not send soldiers to oppress us. If the people of Boston must fight for their liberty, we will help them." These men were not afraid of the king's soldiers. Some of them camped in Charlestown, [Footnote: Charles'town.] a village near Boston. From the hills of Charlestown they could watch and see what the king's soldiers were doing.

They wished to be ready to defend themselves, if the soldiers should try to do them harm. For this reason they had bought some powder and stored it at Concord,[Footnote: Concord (*pro.* kong'krd).] nearly twenty miles away.

When the king's soldiers heard about this powder, they made up their minds to go out and get it for themselves.

Among the watchers at Charlestown was a brave young man named Paul Revere. He was ready to serve his country in any way that he could.

One day a friend of his who lived in Boston came to see him. He came very quietly and secretly, to escape the soldiers.

"I have something to tell you," he said. "Some of the king's soldiers are going to Concord to get the powder that is there. They are getting ready to start this very night."

"Indeed!" said Paul Revere. "They shall get no powder, if I can help it. I will stir up all the farmers between here and Concord, and those fellows will have a hot time of it. But you must help me."

"I will do all that I can," said his friend.

"Well, then," said Paul Revere, "you must go back to Boston and watch. Watch, and as soon as the soldiers are ready to start, hang a lantern in the tower of the old North Church. If they are to cross the river, hang two. I will be here, ready. As soon as I see the light, I will mount my horse and ride out to give the alarm."

And so it was done.

When night came, Paul Revere was at the riverside with his horse. He looked over toward Boston. He knew where the old North Church stood, but he could not see much in the darkness.

Hour after hour he stood and watched. The town seemed very still; but now and then he could hear the beating of a drum or the shouting of some soldier.

The moon rose, and by its light he could see the dim form of the church tower, far away. He heard the clock strike ten. He waited and watched.

The clock struck eleven. He was beginning to feel tired. Perhaps the soldiers had given up their plan.

He walked up and down the river bank, leading his horse behind him; but he kept his eyes turned always toward the dim, dark spot which he knew was the old North Church.

All at once a light flashed out from the tower. "Ah! there it is!" he cried. The soldiers had started.

He spoke to his horse. He put his foot in the stirrup. He was ready to mount.

Then another light flashed clear and bright by the side of the first one. The soldiers would cross the river.

Paul Revere sprang into the saddle. Like a bird let loose, his horse leaped forward. Away they went.

Away they went through the village street and out upon the country road. "Up! up!" shouted Paul Revere. "The soldiers are coming! Up! up! and defend yourselves!"

[Illustration]

The cry awoke the farmers; they sprang from their beds and looked out. They could not see the speeding horse, but they heard the clatter of its hoofs far down the road, and they understood the cry, "Up! up! and defend yourselves!"

"It is the alarm! The redcoats are coming," they said to each other. Then they took their guns, their axes, anything they could find, and hurried out.

So, through the night, Paul Revere rode toward Concord. At every farmhouse and every village he repeated his call.

The alarm quickly spread. Guns were fired. Bells were rung. The people for miles around were roused as though a fire were raging.

The king's soldiers were surprised to find everybody awake along the road. They were angry because their plans had been discovered.

When they reached Concord, they burned the courthouse there.

At Lexington, not far from Concord, there was a sharp fight in which several men were killed. This, in history, is called the Battle of Lexington. It was the beginning of the war called the Revolutionary War. But the king's soldiers did not find the gunpowder. They were glad enough to march back without it. All along the road the farmers were waiting for them. It seemed as if every man in the country was after them. And they did not feel themselves safe until they were once more in Boston.

THE BOY AND THE WOLF

In France there once lived a famous man who was known as the Marquis de Lafayette. [Footnote: Mar'quis de La fa yette'.] When he was a little boy his mother called him Gilbert.

Gilbert de Lafayette's father and grandfather and great–grandfather had all been brave and noble men. He was very proud to think of this, and he wished that he might grow up to be like them.

His home was in the country not far from a great forest. Often, when he was a little lad, he took long walks among the trees with his mother.

"Mother," he would say, "do not be afraid. I am with you, and I will not let anything hurt you."

One day word came that a savage wolf had been seen in the forest. Men said that it was a very large wolf and that it had killed some of the farmers' sheep.

"How I should like to meet that wolf," said little Gilbert.

He was only seven years old, but now all his thoughts were about the savage beast that was in the forest.

"Shall we take a walk this morning?" asked his mother.

"Oh, yes!" said Gilbert. "Perhaps we may see that wolf among the trees. But don't be afraid."

His mother smiled, for she felt quite sure that there was no danger.

They did not go far into the woods. The mother sat down in the shade of a tree and began to read in a new book which she had bought the day before. The boy played on the grass near by.

The sun was warm. The bees were buzzing among the flowers. The small birds were singing softly. Gilbert looked up from his play and saw that his mother was very deeply interested in her book.

"Now for the wolf!" he said to himself.

He walked quickly, but very quietly, down the pathway into the darker woods. He looked eagerly around, but saw only a squirrel frisking among the trees and a rabbit hopping across the road.

Soon he came to a wilder place. There the bushes were very close together and the pathway came to an end. He pushed the bushes aside and went a little farther. How still everything was!

He could see a green open space just beyond; and then the woods seemed to be thicker and darker. "This is just the place for that wolf," he thought.

Then, all at once, he heard footsteps. Something was pushing its way through the bushes. It was coming toward him.

"It's the wolf, I'm sure! It will not see me till it comes very near. Then I will jump out and throw my arms around its neck and choke it to death."

The animal was coming nearer. He could hear its footsteps. He could hear its heavy breathing. He stood very still and waited.

"It will try to bite me," he thought. "Perhaps it will scratch me with its sharp claws. But I will be brave. I will not cry out. I will choke it with my strong arms. Then I will drag it out of the bushes and call mamma to come and see it."

The beast was very close to him now. He could see its shadow as he peeped out through the clusters of leaves. His breath came fast. He planted his feet firmly and made ready to spring.

"How proud mamma will be of her brave boy!"

Ah! there was the wolf! He saw its shaggy head and big round eyes. He leaped from his hiding place and clasped it round its neck.

It did not try to bite or scratch. It did not even growl. But it jumped quickly forward and threw Gilbert upon the ground. Then it ran out into the open space and stopped to gaze at him.

Gilbert was soon on his feet again. He was not hurt at all. He looked at the beast, and—what do you think it was?

[Illustration]

It was not a wolf. It was only a pet calf that had come there to browse among the bushes.

The boy felt very much ashamed. He hurried back to the pathway, and then ran to his mother. Tears were in his eyes; but he tried to look brave. "O Gilbert, where have you been?" said his mother.

Then he told her all that had happened. His lips quivered and he began to cry.

"Never mind, my dear," said his mother. "You were very brave, and it is lucky that the wolf was not there. You faced what you thought was a great danger, and you were not afraid. You are my hero."

When the American people were fighting to free themselves from the rule of the king of England, the Marquis de Lafayette helped them with men and money. He was the friend of Washington. His name is remembered in our country as that of a brave and noble man.

ANOTHER WOLF STORY

I

"WOLF! Wolf! Wolf!"

Three farmers were walking across a field and looking eagerly for tracks in the soft ground. One carried a gun, one had a pitchfork, and the third had an ax.

"Wolf! Wolf! Wolf!" they cried, as they met another farmer coming over the hill.

"Where? where?" he asked.

"We don't know," was the answer, "but we saw her tracks down there by the brook. It's the same old wolf that has been skulking around here all winter."

"She killed three of my lambs last night," said the one whose name was David Brown.

"She's killed as many as twenty since the winter began," said Thomas Tanner.

"How do you know that it is only one beast that does all this mischief?" asked the fourth farmer, whose name was Israel Putnam.

"Because the tracks are always the same," answered David Brown. "They show that three toes have been lost from the left forefoot."

"She's been caught in a trap some time, I guess," said Putnam.

"Samuel Stark saw her the other morning," said Tanner. "He says she was a monster; and she was running straight toward the hills with a little lamb in her mouth. They say she has a family of young wolves up there; and that is why she kills so many lambs."

"Here are the tracks again," said Putnam.

They could be seen very plainly, for here the ground was quite muddy. The four men followed them for some distance, and then lost them on the hillside.

"Let us call the neighbors together and have a grand wolf hunt to– morrow," said Putnam. "We must put an end to this killing of lambs."

All the other men agreed to this, and they parted.

II

The next day twenty men and boys came together for the grand wolf hunt. They tracked the beast to the mouth of a cave, far up on the hills.

They shouted and threw stones into the cave. But the wolf was too wise to show herself. She lay hidden among some rocks, and nothing could make her stir.

"I will fetch her out," said Israel Putnam.

The opening to the cave was only a narrow hole between two rocks. Putnam stooped down and looked in. It was very dark there, and he could not see anything.

Then he tied a rope around his waist and said to his friends, "Take hold of the other end, boys. When I jerk it, then pull me out as quickly as you can." He got down on his hands and knees and crawled into the cave. He crawled very slowly and carefully.

At last he saw something in the darkness that looked like two balls of fire. He knew that these were the eyes of the wolf. The wolf gave a low growl and made ready to meet him.

Putnam gave the rope a quick jerk and his friends pulled him out in great haste. They feared that the wolf was upon him; but he wished only to get his gun.

Soon, with the gun in one hand, he crept back into the cave. The wolf saw him. She growled so loudly that the men and boys outside were frightened. But Putnam was not afraid. He raised his gun and fired at the great beast. When his friends heard the gun they pulled the rope quickly and drew him out. It was no fun to be pulled over the sharp stones in that way; but it was better than to be bitten by the wolf. Putnam loaded his gun again. Then he listened. There was not a sound inside of the cave. Perhaps the wolf was waiting to spring upon him. He crept into the cave for the third time. There were no balls of fire to be seen now. No angry growl was heard. The wolf was dead.

Putnam stayed in the cave so long that his friends began to be alarmed. After a while, however, he gave the rope a quick jerk. Men and boys pulled with all their might; and Putnam and the wolf were drawn out together.

This happened when Israel Putnam was a young man. When the Revolutionary War began he was one of the first to hurry to Boston to help the people defend themselves against the British soldiers. He became famous as one of the bravest and best of the generals who fought to make our country free.

THE HORSESHOE NAILS

I

A blacksmith was shoeing a horse.

"Shoe him quickly, for the king wishes to ride him to battle," said the groom who had brought him.

"Do you think there will be a battle?" asked the blacksmith.

"Most certainly, and very soon, too," answered the man. "The king's enemies are even now advancing, and all are ready for the fight. To– day will decide whether Richard or Henry shall be king of England."

The smith went on with his work. From a bar of iron he made four horseshoes. These he hammered and shaped and fitted to the horse's feet. Then he began to nail them on.

But after he had nailed on two shoes, he found that he had not nails enough for the other two. "I have only six nails," he said, "and it will take a little time to hammer out ten more."

"Oh, well," said the groom, "won't six nails do? Put three in each shoe. I hear the trumpets now. King Richard will be impatient."

"Three nails in each shoe will hold them on," said the smith. "Yes, I think we may risk it."

So he quickly finished the shoeing, and the groom hurried to lead the horse to the king.

II

The battle had been raging for some time. King Richard rode hither and thither, cheering his men and fighting his foes. His enemy, Henry, who wished to be king, was pressing him hard.

Far away, at the other side of the field, King Richard saw his men falling back. Without his help they would soon be beaten. So he spurred his horse to ride to their aid.

He was hardly halfway across the stony field when one of the horse's shoes flew off. The horse was lamed on a rock. Then another shoe came off. The horse stumbled, and his rider was thrown heavily to the ground.

Before the king could rise, his frightened horse, although lame, had galloped away. The king looked, and saw that his soldiers were beaten, and that the battle was everywhere going against him.

[Illustration]

He waved his sword in the air. He shouted, "A horse! A horse! My kingdom for a horse." But there was no horse for him. His soldiers were intent on saving themselves. They could not give him any help.

The battle was lost. King Richard was lost. Henry became king of England.

> "For the want of a nail the shoe was lost;
> For the want of a shoe the horse was lost;
> For the want of a horse the battle was lost;
> For the failure of battle the kingdom was lost;—
> And all for the want of a horseshoe nail."

Richard the Third was one of England's worst kings. Henry, the Duke of Richmond, made war upon him and defeated him in a great battle.

THE LANDLORD'S MISTAKE

When John Adams was president and Thomas Jefferson was vice president of the United States, there was not a railroad in all the world.

People did not travel very much. There were no broad, smooth highways as there are now. The roads were crooked and muddy and rough.

If a man was obliged to go from one city to another, he often rode on horseback. Instead of a trunk for his clothing, he carried a pair of saddlebags. Instead of sitting at his ease in a parlor car, he went jolting along through mud and mire, exposed to wind and weather.

One day some men were sitting by the door of a hotel in Baltimore. As they looked down the street they saw a horseman coming. He was riding very slowly, and both he and his horse were bespattered with mud.

"There comes old Farmer Mossback," said one of the men, laughing. "He's just in from the backwoods."

"He seems to have had a hard time of it," said another; "I wonder where he'll put up for the night."

"Oh, any kind of a place will suit him," answered the landlord. "He's one of those country fellows who can sleep in the haymow and eat with the horses."

The traveler was soon at the door. He was dressed plainly, and, with his reddish–brown hair and mud–bespattered face, looked like a hard–working countryman just in from the backwoods.

"Have you a room here for me?" he asked the landlord.

Now the landlord prided himself upon keeping a first–class hotel, and he feared that his guests would not like the rough–looking traveler. So he answered: "No, sir. Every room is full. The only place I could put you would be in the barn."

"Well, then," answered the stranger, "I will see what they can do for me at the Planters' Tavern, round the corner;" and he rode away.

About an hour later, a well–dressed gentleman came into the hotel and said, "I wish to see Mr. Jefferson."

"Mr. Jefferson!" said the landlord.

"Yes, sir. Thomas Jefferson, the vice president of the United States."

"He isn't here."

"Oh, but he must be. I met him as he rode into town, and he said that he intended to stop at this hotel. He has been here about an hour."

"No, he hasn't. The only man that has been here for lodging to–day was an old clodhopper who was so spattered with mud that you couldn't see the color of his coat. I sent him round to the Planters'."

"Did he have reddish–brown hair, and did he ride a gray horse?"

"Yes, and he was quite tall."

"That was Mr. Jefferson," said the gentleman.

"Mr. Jefferson!" cried the landlord. "Was that the vice president? Here, Dick! build a fire in the best room. Put everything in tiptop order, Sally. What a dunce I was to turn Mr. Jefferson away! He shall have all the rooms in the house, and the ladies' parlor, too, I'll go right round to the Planters' and fetch him back."

So he went to the other hotel, where he found the vice president sitting with some friends in the parlor.

"Mr. Jefferson," he said, "I have come to ask your pardon. You were so bespattered with mud that I thought you were some old farmer. If you'll come back to my house, you shall have the best room in it—yes, all the rooms if you wish. Won't you come?"

"No," answered Mr. Jefferson. "A farmer is as good as any other man; and where there's no room for a farmer, there can be no room for me."

A LESSON IN MANNERS

One morning there was a loud knock at Dean Swift's door. The servant opened it. A man who was outside handed her a fine duck that had lately been killed, and said,—"Here's a present for the Dean. It's from Mr. Boyle."

Then, without another word, he turned and walked away.

A few days afterward the man came again. This time he brought a partridge. "Here's another bird from Mr. Boyle."

Now, Mr. Boyle was a sporting neighbor who spent a good deal of time in shooting. He was a great admirer of Dean Swift, and took pleasure in sending him presents of game.

The third time, the man brought a quail. "Here's something else for the Dean," he said roughly, and tossed it into the servant's arms.

The servant complained to her master. "That fellow has no manners," she said.

"The next time he comes," said the Dean, "let me know, and I will go to the door."

It was not long until the man came with another present. The Dean went to the door.

"Here's a rabbit from Mr. Boyle," said the man.

"See here," said the Dean in a stern voice, "that is not the way to deliver a message here. Just step inside and make believe that you are Dean Swift. I will go out and make believe that I am bringing him a present. I will show you how a messenger ought to behave."

25

"I'll agree to that," said the man; and he stepped inside. The Dean took the rabbit and went out of the house. He walked up the street to the next block. Then he came back and knocked gently at the door.

[Illustration]

The door was opened by the man from Mr. Boyle's. The Dean bowed gracefully and said, "If you please, sir, Mr. Boyle's compliments, and he wishes you to accept of this fine rabbit."

"Oh, thank you," said the man very politely. Then, taking out his purse, he offered the Dean a shilling. "And here is something for your trouble."

The lesson in manners was not forgotten; for, always after that, the man was very polite when he brought his presents. And the Dean also took the hint; for he always remembered to give the man a "tip" for his trouble. Jonathan Swift, often called Dean Swift, was famous as a writer on many subjects. Among other books he wrote "Gulliver's Travels," which you, perhaps, will read some time.

GOING TO SEA

"I should like to be a sailor," said George Washington. "Then I could go to many strange lands and see many wonderful things. And, by and by, I might become the captain of a ship."

He was only fourteen years old.

His older brothers were quite willing that he should go to sea. They said that a bright boy like George would not long be a common sailor. He would soon become a captain and then perhaps a great admiral.

And so the matter was at last settled. George's brothers knew the master of a trading ship who was getting ready to sail to England. He agreed to take the boy with him and teach him how to be a good sailor.

George's mother was very sad. His uncle had written her a letter saying:

"Do not let him go to sea. If he begins as a common sailor, he will never be anything else."

But George had made up his mind to go. He was headstrong and determined. He would not listen to any one who tried to persuade him to stay at home. At last the day came for the ship to sail. It was waiting in the river. A boat was at the landing, ready to take him on board. The little chest that held his clothing had been carried down to the bank. George was in high glee at the thought of going.

"Good–by, mother," he said.

He stood on the doorstep and looked back into the house. He saw the kind faces of those whom he loved. He began to feel very sad.

"Good–by, my dear boy!"

George saw the tears in his mother's eyes. He saw them rolling down her cheeks. He knew that she did not wish him to go. He could not bear to see her grief.

He stood still for a moment, thinking. Then he turned quickly and said, "Mother, I have changed my mind. I will stay at home and do as you wish." Then he called to the black boy, who was waiting at the door, and said, "Tom, run down to the shore and tell them not to put the chest in the boat. Send word to the captain not to wait for me, for I have changed my mind. I am not going to sea."

Who has not heard of George Washington? It has been said of him that he was the "first in war, the first in peace, and first in the hearts of his countrymen." He was our most famous president. He has been called the Father of his Country.

THE SHEPHERD–BOY PAINTER

One day a traveler was walking through a part of Italy where a great many sheep were pasturing. Near the top of a hill he saw a little shepherd boy who was lying on the ground while a flock of sheep and lambs were grazing around him.

As he came nearer he saw that the boy held a charred stick in his hand, with which he was drawing something on a flat rock. The lad was so much interested in his work that he did not see the stranger.

[Illustration]

The stranger bent over him and looked at the picture he had made on the rock. It was the picture of a sheep, and it was drawn so well that the stranger was filled with astonishment.

"What is your name, my boy?" he said.

The lad was startled. He jumped to his feet and looked up at the kind gentleman.

"My name is Giotto," [Footnote: Giotto (*pro.* jot'to).] he answered.

"What is your father's name?"

"Bondone." [Footnote: BON do'na.]

"And whose sheep are these?"

"They belong to the rich man who lives in the big white house there among the trees. My father works in the field, and I take care of the sheep." "How would you like to live with me, Giotto? I would teach you how to draw pictures of sheep and horses, and even of men," said the stranger. The boy's face beamed with delight. "I should like to learn to do that—oh, ever so much!" he answered. "But I must do as father says." "Let us go and ask him," said the stranger.

27

The stranger's name was Cimabue.[Footnote: Cimabue (*pro*. she ma boo'a).] He was the most famous painter of the time. His pictures were known and admired in every city of Italy.

Bondone was surprised when Cimabue offered to take his little boy to Florence and teach him to be a great painter.

"I know that the lad can draw pictures wonderfully well," he said. "He does not like to do anything else. Perhaps he will do well with you. Yes, you may take him."

In the city of Florence [Footnote: Flor'ence.] little Giotto saw some of the finest pictures in the world. He learned so fast that he could soon paint as well as Cimabue himself.

One day Cimabue was painting the picture of a man's face. Night came on before he had finished it. "I will leave it till morning," he said; "then the light will be better."

In the morning, when he looked at the picture, he saw a fly on the man's nose. He tried to brush it off, but it remained there. It was only a painted fly.

"Who has done this?" he cried. He was angry, and yet he was pleased.

Little Giotto came out from a corner, trembling and ashamed. "I did it, master," he said. "It was a good place for a fly, and I never thought of spoiling your picture."

He expected to be punished. But Cimabue only praised him for his great skill. "There are few men who can draw so good a picture of a fly," he said.

This happened six hundred years ago, in the city of Florence in Italy. The shepherd boy became a very famous painter and the friend of many famous men.

TWO GREAT PAINTERS

There was once a painter whose name was Zeuxis. [Footnote: Zeuxis (*pro*. zuke'sis).] He could paint pictures so life–like that they were mistaken for the real things which they represented.

At one time he painted the picture of some fruit which was so real that the birds flew down and pecked at it. This made him very proud of his skill.

"I am the only man in the world who can paint a picture so true to life," he said.

There was another famous artist whose name was Parrhasius. [Footnote: Parrhasius (*pro*. pa ra'shl us).] When he heard of the boast which Zeuxis had made, he said to himself, "I will see what I can do."

So he painted a beautiful picture which seemed to be covered with a curtain. Then he invited Zeuxis to come and see it.

Zeuxis looked at it closely. "Draw the curtain aside and show us the picture," he said.

Parrhasius laughed and answered, "The curtain is the picture."

"Well," said Zeuxis, "you have beaten me this time, and I shall boast no more. I deceived only the birds, but you have deceived me, a painter."

Some time after this, Zeuxis painted another wonderful picture. It was that of a boy carrying a basket of ripe red cherries. When he hung this painting outside of his door, some birds flew down and tried to carry the cherries away.

"Ah! this picture is a failure," he said. "For if the boy had been as well painted as the cherries, the birds would have been afraid to come near him."

THE KING AND THE BEES

One day King Solomon was sitting on his throne, and his great men were standing around him.

Suddenly the door was thrown open and the Queen of Sheba came in.

"O King," she said, "in my own country, far, far away, I have heard much about your power and glory, but much more about your wisdom. Men have told me that there is no riddle so cunning that you can not solve it. Is this true?"

[Illustration]

"It is as you say, O Queen," answered Solomon.

"Well, I have here a puzzle which I think will test your wisdom. Shall I show it to you?"

"Most certainly, O Queen."

Then she held up in each hand a beautiful wreath of flowers. The wreaths were so nearly alike that none of those who were with the king could point out any difference.

"One of these wreaths." said the queen, "is made of flowers plucked from your garden. The other is made of artificial flowers, shaped and colored by a skillful artist. Now, tell me, O King, which is the true, and which is the false?"

The king, for once, was puzzled. He stroked his chin. He looked at the wreaths from every side. He frowned. He bit his lips.

"Which is the true?" the queen again asked.

Still the king did not answer.

"I have heard that you are the wisest man in the world," she said, "and surely this simple thing ought not to puzzle you."

The king moved uneasily on his golden throne. His officers and great men shook their heads. Some would have smiled, if they had dared.

"Look at the flowers carefully," said the queen, "and let us have your answer."

Then the king remembered something. He remembered that close by his window there was a climbing vine filled with beautiful sweet flowers. He remembered that he had seen many bees flying among these flowers and gathering honey from them.

So he said, "Open the window!"

It was opened. The queen was standing quite near to it with the two wreaths still in her hands. All eyes were turned to see why the king had said, "Open the window."

The next moment two bees flew eagerly in. Then came another and another. All flew to the flowers in the queen's right hand. Not one of the bees so much as looked at those in her left hand.

"O Queen of Sheba, the bees have given you my answer," then said Solomon.

And the queen said, "You are wise, King Solomon. You gather knowledge from the little things which common men pass by unnoticed."

King Solomon lived three thousand years ago. He built a great temple in Jerusalem, and was famous for his wisdom.

OUR FIRST GREAT PAINTER

A long time ago there lived, in Pennsylvania, a little boy whose name was Benjamin West.

This boy loved pictures. Indeed, there were few things that he loved more. But he had never seen any pictures except a few small ones in a book. His father and mother were Quakers, and they did not think it was right to spend money for such things. They thought that pictures might take one's mind away from things that were better or more useful.

One day Benjamin's mother had to go to a neighbor's on some errand. So she told Benjamin to stay in the house and take care of his baby sister till she came back.

He was glad to do this; for he loved the baby.

"Yes, mother," he said, "I will watch her every minute. I won't let anything hurt her."

The baby was asleep in her cradle, and he must not make a noise and waken her. For some time he sat very still. He heard the clock ticking. He heard the birds singing. He began to feel a little lonesome.

A fly lighted on the baby's cheek, and he brushed it away. Then he thought what a pretty picture might be made of his sister's sweet face and little hands.

He had no paper, but he knew where there was a smooth board. He had no pencil, but there was a piece of black charcoal on the hearth. How pretty the baby was! He began to draw. The baby smiled but did not wake up.

[Illustration]

As often as he touched the charcoal to the smooth board, the picture grew. Here was her round head, covered with pretty curls. Here was her mouth. Here were her eyes, and here her dainty ears. Here was her fat little neck. Here were her wonderful hands.

So busy was he with the drawing that he did not think of anything else. He heard neither the clock nor the birds. He did not even hear his mother's footsteps as she came into the room. He did not hear her soft breathing as she stood over him and watched him finish the wonderful drawing. "O Benjamin! what has thee been doing?" she cried.

The lad sprang up alarmed.

"It's only a picture of the baby, mother," he said.

"A picture of the baby! Oh, wonderful! It looks just like her!"

The good woman was so overjoyed that she caught him in her arms and kissed him. Then suddenly she began to wonder whether this was right.

"Benjamin, how did thee learn to draw such a picture?" she asked.

"I didn't learn," he answered. "I just did it. I couldn't help but do it."

When Benjamin's father came home, his mother showed him the picture. "It looks just like her, doesn't it?" she said. "But I am afraid. I don't know what to think. Does thee suppose that it is very wrong for Benjamin to do such a thing?"

The father did not answer. He turned the picture this way and that, and looked at it from every side. He compared it with the baby's pretty face. Then he handed it back to his wife and said:—

"Put it away. It may be that the hand of the Lord is in this."

Several weeks afterward, there came a visitor to the home of the Wests. It was a good old Friend, whom everybody loved—a–white–haired, pleasant–faced minister, whose words were always wise.

Fifty Famous People

Benjamin's parents showed him the picture. They told him how the lad was always trying to draw something. And they asked what they should do about it.

The good minister looked at the picture for a long time. Then he called little Benjamin to him. He put his hands on the lad's head and said:—

"This child has a wonderful gift. We cannot understand it nor the reason of it. Let us trust that great good may come from it, and that Benjamin West may grow up to be an honor to our country and the world."

And the words of the old minister came true. The pictures of Benjamin West made him famous. He was the first great American painter.

THE YOUNG SCOUT

When Andrew Jackson was a little boy he lived with his mother in South Carolina. He was eight years old when he heard about the ride of Paul Revere and the famous fight at Lexington.

It was then that the long war, called the Revolutionary War, began. The king's soldiers were sent into every part of the country. The people called them the British. Some called them "red–coats."

There was much fighting; and several great battles took place between the British and the Americans.

At last Charleston, in South Carolina, was taken by the British. Andrew Jackson was then a tall white–haired boy, thirteen years old.

"I am going to help drive those red–coated British out of the country," he said to his mother.

Then, without another word, he mounted his brother's little farm horse and rode away. He was not old enough to be a soldier, but he could be a scout—and a good scout he was.

He was very tall—as tall as a man. He was not afraid of anything. He was strong and ready for every duty.

One day as he was riding through the woods, some British soldiers saw him. They quickly surrounded him and made him their prisoner.

"Come with us," they said, "and we will teach you that the king's soldiers are not to be trifled with."

They took him to the British camp.

"What is your name, young rebel?" said the British captain.

"Andy Jackson."

"Well, Andy Jackson, get down here and clean the mud from my boots."

Andrew's gray eyes blazed as he stood up straight and proud before the haughty captain.

"Sir," he said, "I am a prisoner of war, and demand to be treated as such."

"You rebel!" shouted the captain. "Down with you, and clean those boots at once."

The slim, tall boy seemed to grow taller, as he answered, "I'll not be the servant of any Englishman that ever lived."

[Illustration]

The captain was very angry. He drew his sword to hit the boy with its flat side. Andrew threw out his hand and received an ugly gash across the knuckles.

Some other officers, who had seen the whole affair, cried out to the captain, "Shame! He is a brave boy. He deserves to be treated as a gentleman."

Andrew was not held long as a prisoner. The British soldiers soon returned to Charleston, and he was allowed to go home.

In time, Andrew Jackson became a very great man. He was elected to Congress, he was chosen judge of the supreme court of Tennessee, he was appointed general in the army, and lastly he was for eight years the president of the United States.

THE LAD WHO RODE SIDESADDLE

When Daniel Webster was a child he lived in the country, far from any city. He was not strong enough to work on the farm like his brothers; but he loved books and study.

He was very young when he was first sent to school. The schoolhouse was two or three miles from home, but he did not mind the long walk through the woods and over the hills.

He soon learned all that his teacher could teach; for he was bright and quick, and had a good memory.

His father hoped that Daniel would grow up to be a wise and famous man. "But," said he, "no man can rightly succeed without an education."

So it was decided that the boy should go to some school where he might be prepared for college.

One evening his father said to him, "Daniel, you must be up early in the morning. You are going to Exeter with me."

"To Exeter, father!" said Daniel.

"Yes, to Exeter. I am going to put you in the academy there."

The academy at Exeter was a famous school for preparing boys for college. It is still a famous school. But Daniel's father did not say anything about college.

There were no railroads at that time, and Exeter was nearly fifty miles away. Daniel and his father would ride there on horseback.

Early in the morning two horses were brought to the door. One was Mr. Webster's horse; the other was an old gray nag with a lady's sidesaddle on its back.

"Who is going to ride that nag?" asked Daniel.

"Young Dan Webster," answered his father.

"But I don't want a sidesaddle. I'm not a lady."

"I understand," said Mr. Webster. "But our neighbor, Johnson, is sending the nag to Exeter for the use of a lady who is to ride back with me. He does me a favor by allowing you to ride on the animal, and I do him a favor by taking care of it."

"But won't it look rather funny for me to ride to Exeter on a sidesaddle?"

"Well, if a lady can ride on it, perhaps Dan Webster can do as much."

And so they set out on their journey to Exeter. Mr. Webster rode in front, and Daniel, on the old gray nag, followed behind. The roads were muddy, and they went slowly. It took them two days to reach Exeter.

The people whom they met gazed at them and wondered who they could be. They scarcely noticed the sidesaddle; they noticed only the boy's dark eyes and his strong, noble face.

His clothes were of homemade stuff; his shoes were coarse and heavy; he had no gloves on his hands; he was awkward and bashful.

Yet there was something in his manner and voice that caused everybody to admire him.

Daniel Webster lived to become a famous orator and a great statesman. He was honored at home and abroad.

THE WHISPERERS

"Boys, what did I tell you?"

The schoolmaster spoke angrily. He was in trouble because his scholars would not study. Whenever his back was turned, they were sure to begin whispering to one another.

"Girls, stop your whispering, I say."

But still they would whisper, and he could not prevent it. The afternoon was half gone, and the trouble was growing. Then the master thought of a plan.

"Children," he said, "we are going to play a new game. The next one that whispers must come out and stand in the middle of the floor. He must stand there until he sees some one else whisper. Then he will tell me, and the one whom he names must come and take his place. He, in turn, will watch and report the first one that he sees whisper. And so we will keep the game going till it is time for school to be dismissed. The boy or girl who is standing at that time will be punished for all of you."

"What will the punishment be, Mr. Johnson?" asked a bold, bad boy. "A good thrashing," answered the master. He was tired, he was vexed, he hardly knew what he said.

The children thought the new game was very funny. First, Tommy Jones whispered to Billy Brown and was at once called out to stand on the floor. Within less than two minutes, Billy saw Mary Green whispering, and she had to take his place. Mary looked around and saw Samuel Miller asking his neighbor for a pencil, and Samuel was called. And so the fun went on until the clock showed that it lacked only ten minutes till school would be dismissed.

Then all became very good and very careful, for no one wished to be standing at the time of dismissal. They knew that the master would be as good as his word. The clock ticked loudly, and Tommy Jones, who was standing up for the fourth time, began to feel very uneasy. He stood on one leg and then on the other, and watched very closely; but nobody whispered. Could it be possible that he would receive that thrashing? Suddenly, to his great joy he saw little Lucy Martin lean over her desk and whisper to the girl in front of her. Now Lucy was the pet of the school. Everybody loved her, and this was the first time she had whispered that day. But Tommy didn't care for that. He wished to escape the punishment, and so he called out, "Lucy Martin!" and went proudly to his seat.

Little Lucy had not meant to whisper. There was something which she wished very much to know before going home, and so, without thinking, she had leaned over and whispered just three little words. With tears in her eyes she went out and stood in the whisperer's place.

[Illustration]

She was very much ashamed and hurt, for it was the first time that she had ever been in disgrace at school. The other girls felt sorry that she should suffer for so small a fault. The boys looked at her and wondered if the master would really be as good as his word.

The clock kept on ticking. It lacked only one minute till the bell would strike the time for dismissal. What a shame that dear, gentle Lucy should be punished for all those unruly boys and girls!

Then, suddenly, an awkward half–grown boy who sat right in front of the master's desk turned squarely around and whispered to Tommy Jones, three desks away.

Everybody saw him. Little Lucy Martin saw him through her tears, but said nothing. Everybody was astonished, for that boy was the best scholar in the school, and he had never been known to break a rule.

It lacked only half a minute now. The awkward boy turned again and whispered so loudly that even the master could not help hearing: "Tommy, you deserve a thrashing!"

"Elihu Burritt, take your place on the floor," said the master sternly. The awkward boy stepped out quickly, and little Lucy Martin returned to her seat sobbing. At the same moment the bell struck and school was dismissed.

After all the others had gone home, the master took down his long birch rod and said: "Elihu, I suppose I must be as good as my word. But tell me why you so deliberately broke the rule against whispering."

"I did it to save little Lucy," said the awkward boy, standing up very straight and brave. "I could not bear to see her punished."

"Elihu, you may go home," said the master.

All this happened many years ago in New Britain, Connecticut. Elihu Burritt was a poor boy who was determined to learn. He worked many years as a blacksmith and studied books whenever he had a spare moment. He learned many languages and became known all over the world as "The Learned Blacksmith."

HOW A PRINCE LEARNED TO READ

I

A thousand years ago boys and girls did not learn to read. Books were very scarce and very precious, and only a few men could read them.

Each book was written with a pen or a brush. The pictures were painted by hand, and some of them were very beautiful. A good book would sometimes cost as much as a good house.

In those times there were even some kings who could not read. They thought more of hunting and fighting than of learning.

There was one such king who had four sons, Ethelbald, Ethelbert, Ethelred, and Alfred.[Footnote: Eth'el bald, Eth'el bert, Eth'el red, Al'fred.] The three older boys were sturdy, half–grown lads; the youngest, Alfred, was a slender, fair–haired child.

One day when they were with their mother, she showed them a wonderful book that some rich friend had given her. She turned the leaves and showed them the strange letters. She showed them the beautiful pictures, and told them how they had been drawn and painted.

They admired the book very much, for they had never seen anything like it. "But the best part of it is the story which it tells," said their mother. "If you could only read, you might learn that story and enjoy it. Now I have a mind to give this book to one of you"

"Will you give it to me, mother?" asked little Alfred.

"I will give it to the one who first learns to read in it" she answered.

"I am sure I would rather have a good bow with arrows" said Ethelred.

"And I would rather have a young hawk that has been trained to hunt" said Ethelbert.

"If I were a priest or a monk" said Ethelbald, "I would learn to read. But I am a prince, and it is foolish for princes to waste their time with such things."

"But I should like to know the story which this book tells," said Alfred.

II

A few weeks passed by. Then, one morning, Alfred went into his mother's room with a smiling, joyous face.

"Mother," he said, "will you let me see that beautiful book again?"

His mother unlocked her cabinet and took the precious volume from its place of safe keeping.

Alfred opened it with careful fingers. Then he began with the first word on the first page and read the first story aloud without making one mistake.

"O my child, how did you learn to do that?" cried his mother.

"I asked the monk, Brother Felix, to teach me," said Alfred. "And every day since you showed me the book, he has given me a lesson. It was no easy thing to learn these letters and how they are put together to make words. Now, Brother Felix says I can read almost as well as he."

"How wonderful!" said his mother.

"How foolish!" said Ethelbald.

[Illustration]

"You will be a good monk when you grow up," said Ethelred, with a sneer.

But his mother kissed him and gave him the beautiful book. "The prize is yours, Alfred," she said. "I am sure that whether you grow up to be a monk or a king, you will be a wise and noble man."

And Alfred did grow up to become the wisest and noblest king that England ever had. In history he is called Alfred the Great.

"READ, AND YOU WILL KNOW"

"Mother, what are the clouds made of? Why does the rain fall? Where does all the rain water go? What good does it do?"

Little William Jones was always asking questions.

"I want to know," he said; "I want to know everything."

At first his mother tried to answer all his questions. But after he had learned to read, she taught him to look in books for that which he wished to know.

"Mother, what makes the wind blow?"

"Read, and you will know, my child."

"Who lives on the other side of the world?"

"Read, and you will know."

"Why is the sky so blue?"

"Read, and you will know."

"Oh, mother, I would like to know everything."

"You can never know everything, my child. But you can learn many things from books."

"Yes, mother, I will read and then I will know."

He was a very little boy, but before he was three years old he could read quite well. When eight years of age he was the best scholar at the famous school at Harrow. He was always reading, learning, inquiring.

"I want to know; I want to know," he kept saying.

"Read, and you will know," said his mother. "Read books that are true. Read about things that are beautiful and good. Read in order to become wise.

"Do not waste your time in reading foolish books. Do not read bad books, they will make you bad. No book is worth reading that does not make you better or wiser."

And so William Jones went on reading and learning. He became one of the most famous scholars in the world. The king of England made him a knight and called him Sir William Jones. Sir William Jones lived nearly two hundred years ago. He was noted for his great knowledge, the most of which he had obtained from books. It is said that he could speak and write forty languages.

THE YOUNG CUPBEARER

I

Long, long ago, there lived in Persia a little prince whose name was Cyrus. [Footnote: Cyrus (*pro.* si'rus).]

He was not petted and spoiled like many other princes. Although his father was a king, Cyrus was brought up like the son of a common man.

He knew how to work with his hands. He ate only the plainest food. He slept on a hard bed. He learned to endure hunger and cold.

When Cyrus was twelve years old he went with his mother to Media to visit his grandfather. His grandfather, whose name was Astyages, [Footnote: Astyages (*pro.* as ti'a jeez).] was king of Media, and very rich and powerful.

Cyrus was so tall and strong and handsome that his grandfather was very proud of him. He wished the lad to stay with him in Media. He therefore gave him many beautiful gifts and everything that could please a prince. One day King Astyages planned to make a great feast for the lad. The tables were to be laden with all kinds of food. There was to be music and dancing; and Cyrus was to invite as many guests as he chose. The hour for the feast came. Everything was ready. The servants were there, dressed in fine uniforms. The musicians and dancers were in their places. But no guests came.

"How is this, my dear boy?" asked the king. "The feast is ready, but no one has come to partake of it."

"That is because I have not invited any one," said Cyrus." In Persia we do not have such feasts. If any one is hungry, he eats some bread and meat, with perhaps a few cresses, and that is the end of it. We never go to all this trouble and expense of making a fine dinner in order that our friends may eat what is not good for them."

King Astyages did not know whether to be pleased or displeased.

"Well," said he, "all these rich foods that were prepared for the feast are yours. What will you do with them?"

"I think I will give them to our friends," said Cyrus.

So he gave one portion to the king's officer who had taught him to ride. Another portion he gave to an old servant who waited upon his grandfather. And the rest he divided among the young women who took care of his mother.

II

The king's cupbearer, Sarcas, was very much offended because he was not given a share of the feast. The king also wondered why this man, who was his favorite, should be so slighted.

"Why didn't you give something to Sarcas?" he asked.

"Well, truly," said Cyrus, "I do not like him. He is proud and overbearing. He thinks that he makes a fine figure when he waits on you." "And so he does," said the king. "He is very skillful as a cupbearer." "That may be so," answered Cyrus, "but if you will let me be your cupbearer tomorrow, I think I can serve you quite as well."

King Astyages smiled. He saw that Cyrus had a will of his own, and this pleased him very much.

"I shall be glad to see what you can do," he said. "Tomorrow, you shall be the king's cupbearer."

III

You would hardly have known the young prince when the time came for him to appear before his grandfather. He was dressed in the rich uniform of the cupbearer, and he came forward with much dignity and grace.

He carried a white napkin upon his arm, and held the cup of wine very daintily with three of his fingers.

[Illustration]

His manners were perfect. Sarcas himself could not have served the king half so well.

"Bravo! bravo!" cried his mother, her eyes sparkling with pride.

"You have done well" said his grandfather. "But you neglected one important thing. It is the rule and custom of the cupbearer to pour out a little of the wine and taste it before handing the cup to me. This you forgot to do."

"Indeed, grandfather, I did not forget it," answered Cyrus.

"Then why didn't you do it?" asked his mother.

"Because I believed there was poison in the wine."

"Poison, my boy!" cried King Astyages, much alarmed. "Poison! poison!"

"Yes, grandfather, poison. For the other day, when you sat at dinner with your officers, I noticed that the wine made you act queerly. After the guests had drunk quite a little of it, they began to talk foolishly and sing loudly; and some of them went to sleep. And you, grandfather, were as bad as the rest. You forgot that you were king. You forgot all your good manners. You tried to dance and fell upon the floor. I am afraid to drink anything that makes men act in that way."

"Didn't you ever see your father behave so?" asked the king.

"No, never," said Cyrus. "He does not drink merely to be drinking. He drinks to quench his thirst, and that is all."

When Cyrus became a man, he succeeded his father as king of Persia; he also succeeded his grandfather Astyages as king of Media. He was a very wise and powerful ruler, and he made his country the greatest of any that was then known. In history he is commonly called Cyrus the Great.

THE SONS OF THE CALIPH

There was a caliph of Persia whose name was Al Mamoun. [Footnote: Al Mam'oun] He had two sons whom he wished to become honest and noble men. So he employed a wise man whose name was Al Farra to be their teacher. One day, after lesson hours, Al Farra rose to go out of the house. The two boys saw him and ran to fetch his shoes. For in that country, people never wear shoes in the house, but take them off at the door. The two boys ran for the teacher's shoes, and each claimed the honor of carrying them to him. But they dared not quarrel and at last agreed that each should carry one shoe. Thus the honor would be divided. When the caliph heard of this he sent for Al Farra and asked him, "Who is the most honored of men?"

The teacher answered, "I know of no man who is more honored than yourself."

"No, no," said the caliph. "It is the man who rose to go out, and two young princes contended for the honor of giving him his shoes but at last agreed that each should offer him one."

Al Farra answered, "Sir, I should have forbidden them to do this, but I feared to discourage them. I hope that I shall never do anything to make them careless of their duties."

"Well," said the caliph, "if you had forbidden them thus to honor you, I should have declared you in the wrong. They did nothing that was beneath the dignity of princes. Indeed, they honored themselves by honoring you." Al Farra bowed low, but said nothing; and the caliph went on. "No young man nor boy," said he, "can be so high in rank as to neglect three great duties: he must respect his ruler, he must love and obey his father, and he must honor his teacher."

Then he called the two young princes to him, and as a reward for their noble conduct, filled their pockets with gold.

THE BOY AND THE ROBBERS

In Persia, when Cyrus the Great was king, boys were taught to tell the truth. This was one of their first lessons at home and at school.

"None but a coward will tell a falsehood," said the father of young Otanes. [Footnote: Otanes (*pro.* o ta'n ez).]

"Truth is beautiful. Always love it," said his mother.

When Otanes was twelve years old, his parents wished to send him to a distant city to study in a famous school that was there. It would be a long journey and a dangerous one. So it was arranged that the boy should travel with a small company of merchants who were going to the same place. "Good–by, Otanes! Be always brave and truthful," said his father. "Farewell, my child! Love that which is beautiful. Despise that which is base," said his mother.

The little company began its long journey. Some of the men rode on camels, some on horses. They went but slowly, for the sun was hot and the way was rough.

Suddenly, towards evening, a band of robbers swooped down upon them. The merchants were not fighting men. They could do nothing but give up all their goods and money.

"Well, boy, what have you got?" asked one of the robbers, as he pulled Otanes from his horse.

"Forty pieces of gold" answered the lad.

The robber laughed. He had never heard of a boy with so much money as that.

"That is a good story" he said. "Where do you carry your gold?"

"It is in my hat, underneath the lining," answered Otanes.

"Oh, well! You can't make me believe that," said the robber; and he hurried away to rob one of the rich merchants.

Soon another came up and said, "My boy, do you happen to have any gold about you?"

"Yes! Forty pieces, in my hat, said Otanes.

"You are a brave lad to be joking with robbers" said the man; and he also hurried on to a more promising field.

At length the chief of the band called to Otanes and said, "Young fellow, have you anything worth taking?"

Otanes answered, "I have already told two of your men that I have forty pieces of gold in my hat. But they wouldn't believe me."

"Take off your hat," said the chief.

[Illustration]

The boy obeyed. The chief tore out the lining and found the gold hidden beneath it.

"Why did you tell us where to find it?" he asked. "No one would have thought that a child like you had gold about him."

"If I had answered your questions differently, I should have told a lie," said Otanes; "and none but cowards tell lies"

The robber chief was struck by this answer. He thought of the number of times that he himself had been a coward. Then he said, "You are a brave boy, and you may keep your gold. Here it is. Mount your horse, and my own men will ride with you and see that you reach the end of your journey in safety."

Otanes, in time, became one of the famous men of his country. He was the advisor and friend of two of the kings who succeeded Cyrus.

A LESSON IN JUSTICE

Alexander [Footnote: Al ex an'der.] the king of Macedon, [Footnote: Macedon (pro. mas'e don).] wished to become the master of the whole world. He led his armies through many countries. He plundered cities, he burned towns, he destroyed thousands of lives.

At last, far in the East, he came to a land of which he had never heard. The people there knew nothing about war and conquest. Although they were rich, they lived simply and were at peace with all the world.

The shah, or ruler of these people, went out to meet Alexander and welcome him to their country. He led the great king to his palace and begged that he would dine with him.

When they were seated at the table the servants of the shah stood by to serve the meal. They brought in what seemed to be fruits, nuts, cakes, and other delicacies; but when Alexander would eat he found that everything was made of gold.

"What!" said he, "do you eat gold in this country?"

"We ourselves eat only common food," answered the shah. "But we have heard that it was the desire for gold which caused you to leave your own country; and so, we wish to satisfy your appetite."

"It was not for gold that I came here," said Alexander. "I came to learn the customs of your people."

"Very well, then," said the shah, "stay with me a little while and observe what you can."

While the shah and the king were talking, two countrymen came in. "My lord," said one, "we have had a disagreement, and wish you to settle the matter."

"Tell me about it," said the shah.

"Well, it is this way," answered the man: "I bought a piece of ground from this neighbor of mine, and paid him a fair price for it. Yesterday, when I was digging in it, I found a box full of gold and jewels. This treasure does not belong to me, for I bought only the ground; but when I offered it to my neighbor he refused it."

The second man then spoke up and said, "It is true that I sold him the ground, but I did not reserve anything he might find in it. The treasure is not mine, and therefore I am unwilling to take it."

The shah sat silent for a while, as if in thought. Then he said to the first man, "Have you a son?"

"Yes, a young man of promise," was the answer.

The shah turned to the second man: "Have you a daughter?"

"I have," answered the man, "—a beautiful girl."

"Well, then, this is my judgment. Let the son marry the daughter, if both agree, and give them the treasure as a wedding portion."

Alexander listened with great interest. "You have judged wisely and rightly," said he to the shah, "but in my own country we should have done differently."

"What would you have done?"

"Well, we should have thrown both men into prison, and the treasure would have been given to the king."

"And is that what you call justice?" asked the shah.

"We call it policy," said Alexander.

"Then let me ask you a question," said the shah. "Does the sun shine in your country?"

"Surely."

"Does the rain fall there?"

"Oh, yes!"

"Is it possible! But are there any gentle, harmless animals in your fields?"

"A great many."

"Then," said the shah, "it must be that the sun shines and the rain falls for the sake of these poor beasts; for men so unjust do not deserve such blessings."

THE GENERAL AND THE FOX

There was once a famous Greek general whose name was Aristomenes. [Footnote: Aristomenes (*pro.* ar is tom'e neez).] He was brave and wise; and his countrymen loved him.

Once, however, in a great battle with the Spartans, his army was beaten and he was taken prisoner.

In those days, people had not learned to be kind to their enemies. In war, they were savage and cruel; for war always makes men so.

The Spartans hated Aristomenes. He had given them a great deal of trouble, and they wished to destroy him.

On a mountain near their city, there was a narrow chasm or hole in the rocks. It was very deep, and there was no way to climb out of it.

The Spartans said to one another, "Let us throw this fellow into the rocky chasm. Then we may be sure that he will never trouble us again."

So a party of soldiers led him up into the mountain and placed him on the edge of the yawning hole in the rocks. "See the place to which we send all our enemies," they said. And they threw him in.

No one knows how he escaped being dashed to pieces. Some of the Greeks said that an eagle caught him in her beak and carried him unharmed to the bottom. But that is not likely.

I think that he must have fallen upon some bushes and vines that grew in some parts of the chasm. At any rate he was not hurt much.

He groped around in the dim light, but could not find any way of escape. The rocky walls surrounded him on every side. There was no place where he could set his foot to climb out.

For three days he lay in his strange prison. He grew weak from hunger and thirst. He expected to die from starvation.

Suddenly he was startled by a noise close by him. Something was moving among the rocks at the bottom of the chasm. He watched quietly, and soon saw a large fox coming towards him.

He lay quite still till the animal was very near. Then he sprang up quickly and seized it by the tail.

The frightened fox scampered away as fast as it could; and Aristomenes followed, clinging to its tail. It ran into a narrow cleft which he had not seen before, and then through a long, dark passage which was barely large enough for a man's body.

Aristomenes held on. At last he saw a ray of light far ahead of him. It was the sunlight streaming in at the entrance to the passage. But soon the way became too narrow for his body to pass through. What should he do? He let go of the fox, and it ran out. Then with great labor he began to widen the passageway. Here the rocks were smaller, and he soon loosened them enough to allow him to squeeze through. In a short time he was free and in the open air.

Some days after this the Spartans heard strange news: "Aristomenes is again at the head of the Greek army." They could not believe it.

THE BOMB

Did you ever hear of King Charles the Twelfth, of Sweden? He lived two hundred years ago, and was famous for his courage in defending his country.

One day he was in the midst of a great battle. The small house in which he had taken shelter was almost between the two armies.

He called to one of his officers and bade him sit down and write a short order for him.

The officer began to write, but just as he finished the first word, a bomb came through the roof of the house and struck the floor close by him. He dropped the pen and sprang to his feet. He was pale with fear. "What is the matter?" asked the king.

"Oh, sir," he answered, "the bomb! the bomb!"

"Yes, I see," said the king. "But what has the bomb to do with what I wish you to write? Sit down, and take your pen. When your country is in danger, you should forget your own safety."

A STORY OF OLD ROME

There was a great famine in Rome. The summer had been very dry and the corn crop had failed. There was no bread in the city. The people were starving.

One day, to the great joy of all, some ships arrived from another country. These ships were loaded with corn. Here was food enough for all.

The rulers of the city met to decide what should be done with the corn.

"Divide it among the poor people who need it so badly," said some. "Let it be a free gift to them from the city."

But one of the rulers was not willing to do this. His name was Coriolanus, [Footnote: Co ri o la'nus.] and he was very rich.

"These people are poor because they have been too lazy to work," he said. "They do not deserve any gifts from the city. Let those who wish any corn bring money and buy it."

When the people heard about this speech of the rich man, Coriolanus, they were very angry.

"He is no true Roman," said some.

"He is selfish and unjust," said others.

"He is an enemy to the poor. Kill him! kill him!" cried the mob. They did not kill him, but they drove him out of the city and bade him never return.

Coriolanus made his way to the city of Antium, [Footnote: Antium (*pro.* an'shi um).] which was not far from Rome. The people of Antium were enemies of the Romans and had often been at war with them. So they welcomed Coriolanus very kindly and made him the general of their army.

Coriolanus began at once to make ready for war against Rome. He persuaded other towns near Antium to send their soldiers to help him.

Soon, at the head of a very great army, he marched toward the city which had once been his home. The rude soldiers of Antium overran all the country around Rome. They burned the villages and farmhouses. They filled the land with terror.

Coriolanus pitched his camp quite near to the city. His army was the greatest that the Romans had ever seen. They knew that they were helpless before so strong an enemy.

"Surrender your city to me," said Coriolanus. "Agree to obey the laws that I shall make for you. Do this, or I will burn Rome and destroy all its people."

The Romans answered, "We must have time to think of this matter. Give us a few days to learn what sort of laws you will make for us, and then we will say whether we can submit to them or not."

"I will give you thirty days to consider the matter," said Coriolanus.

Then he told them what laws he would require them to obey. These laws were so severe that all said, "It will be better to die at once."

At the end of the thirty days, four of the city's rulers went out to beg him to show mercy to the people of Rome. These rulers were old men, with wise faces and long white beards. They went out bareheaded and very humble.

Coriolanus would not listen to them. He drove them back with threats, and told them that they should expect no mercy from him; but he agreed to give them three more days to consider the matter.

The next day, all the priests and learned men went out to beg for mercy. These were dressed in their long flowing robes, and all knelt humbly before him. But he drove them back with scornful words.

On the last day, the great army which Coriolanus had led from Antium was drawn up in battle array. It was ready to march upon the city and destroy it.

All Rome was in terror. There seemed to be no way to escape the anger of this furious man.

Then the rulers, in their despair, said, "Let us go up to the house where Coriolanus used to live when he was one of us. His mother and his wife are still there. They are noble women, and they love Rome. Let us ask them to go out and beg our enemy to have mercy upon us. His heart will be hard indeed if he can refuse his mother and his wife."

The two noble women were willing to do all that they could to save their city. So, leading his little children by the hand, they went out to meet Coriolanus. Behind them followed a long procession of the women of Rome. Coriolanus was in his tent. When he saw his mother and his wife and his children, he was filled with joy. But when they made known their errand, his face darkened, and he shook his head.

For a long time his mother pleaded with him. For a long time his wife begged him to be merciful. His little children clung to his knees and spoke loving words to him.

At last, he could hold out no longer. "O mother," he said, "you have saved your country, but have lost your son!" Then he commanded his army to march back to the city of Antium.

[Illustration]

Rome was saved; but Coriolanus could never return to his home, his mother, his wife and children. He was lost to them.

SAVED BY A DOLPHIN

In the city of Corinth [Footnote: Cor'inth.] there once lived a wonderful musician whose name was Arion. [Footnote: A r_i'on.] No other person could play on the lyre or sing so sweetly as he; and the songs which he composed were famous in many lands.

Fifty Famous People

The king of Corinth was his friend. The people of Corinth never grew tired of praising his sweet music.

One summer he went over the sea to Italy; for his name was well known there, and many people wished to hear him sing.

He visited several cities, and in each place he was well paid for his music.

At last, having become quite rich, he decided to go home. There was a ship just ready to sail for Corinth, and the captain agreed to take him as a passenger.

The sea was rough. The ship was driven far out of her course. Many days passed before they came in sight of land.

The sailors were rude and unruly. The captain himself had been a robber.

When they heard that Arion had a large sum of money with him they began to make plans to get it.

"The easiest way," said the captain, "is to throw him overboard. Then there will be no one to tell tales."

Arion overheard them plotting.

"You may take everything that I have," he said, "if you will only spare my life."

But they had made up their minds to get rid of him. They feared to spare him lest he should report the matter to the king.

"Your life we will not spare," they said; "but we will give you the choice of two things. You must either jump overboard into the sea or be slain with your own sword. Which shall it be?"

"I shall jump overboard," said Arion, "but I pray that you will first grant me a favor."

"What is it?" asked the captain.

"Allow me to sing to you my latest and best song. I promise that as soon as it is finished I will leap into the sea."

The sailors agreed; for they were anxious to hear the musician whose songs were famous all over the world.

[Illustration]

Arion dressed himself in his finest clothing. He took his stand on the forward deck, while the robber sailors stood in a half circle before him, anxious to listen to his song.

He touched his lyre and began to play the accompaniment. Then he sang a wonderful song, so sweet, so lively, so touching, that many of the sailors were moved to tears.

And now they would have spared him; but he was true to his promise,— as soon as the song was finished, he threw himself headlong into the sea.

The sailors divided his money among themselves; and the ship sailed on. In a short time they reached Corinth in safety, and the king sent an officer to bring the captain and his men to the palace.

"Are you lately from Italy?" he asked.

"We are," they answered.

"What news can you give me concerning my friend Arion, the sweetest of all musicians?"

"He was well and happy when we left Italy," they answered. "He has a mind to spend the rest of his life in that country."

Hardly had they spoken these words when the door opened and Arion himself stood before them. He was dressed just as they had seen him when he jumped into the sea. They were so astonished that they fell upon their knees before the king and confessed their crime.

Now, how was Arion saved from drowning when he leaped overboard?

Old story–tellers say that he alighted on the back of a large fish, called a dolphin, which had been charmed by his music and was swimming near the ship. The dolphin carried him with great speed to the nearest shore. Then, full of joy, the musician hastened to Corinth, not stopping even to change his dress.

He told his wonderful story to the king; but the king would not believe him.

"Wait," said he, "till the ship arrives, and then we shall know the truth." Three hours later, the ship came into port, as you have already learned. Other people think that the dolphin which saved Arion was not a fish, but a ship named the *Dolphin*. They say that Arion, being a good swimmer, kept himself afloat until this ship happened to pass by and rescued him from the waves.

You may believe the story that you like best. The name of Arion is still remembered as that of a most wonderful musician.

"LITTLE BROTHERS OF THE AIR"

The man of whom I am now going to tell you was famous, not for his wealth or his power or his deeds in war, but for his great gentleness. He lived more than seven hundred years ago in a quaint little town of Italy. His name was Francis, and because of his goodness, all men now call him St. Francis.

[Illustration]

Very kind and loving was St. Francis—kind and loving not only to men but to all living things. He spoke of the birds as his little brothers of the air, and he could never bear to see them harmed.

At Christmas time he scattered crumbs of bread under the trees, so that the tiny creatures could feast and be happy.

Once when a boy gave him a pair of doves which he had snared, St. Francis had a nest made for them, and the mother bird laid her eggs in it.

By and by, the eggs hatched, and a nestful of young doves grew up. They were so tame that they sat on the shoulders of St. Francis and ate from his hand.

And many other stories are told of this man's great love and pity for the timid creatures which lived in the fields and woods.

One day as he was walking among the trees the birds saw him and flew down to greet him. They sang their sweetest songs to show how much they loved him. Then, when they saw that he was about to speak, they nestled softly in the grass and listened.

"O little birds," he said, "I love you, for you are my brothers and sisters of the air. Let me tell you something, my little brothers, my little sisters: You ought always to love God and praise Him.

"For think what He has given you. He has given you wings with which to fly through the air. He has given you clothing both warm and beautiful. He has given you the air in which to move and have homes.

"And think of this, O little brothers: you sow not, neither do you reap, for God feeds you. He gives you the rivers and the brooks from which to drink. He gives you the mountains and the valleys where you may rest. He gives you the trees in which to build your nests.

"You toil not, neither do you spin, yet God takes care of you and your little ones. It must be, then, that He loves you. So, do not be ungrateful, but sing His praises and thank Him for his goodness toward you."

Then the saint stopped speaking and looked around him. All the birds sprang up joyfully. They spread their wings and opened their mouths to show that they understood his words.

And when he had blessed them, all began to sing; and the whole forest was filled with sweetness and joy because of their wonderful melodies.

A CLEVER SLAVE

A long time ago there lived a poor slave whose name was Aesop. [Footnote: Aesop (*pro*. e'sop).] He was a small man with a large head and long arms. His face was white, but very homely. His large eyes were bright and snappy.

When Aesop was about twenty years old his master lost a great deal of money and was obliged to sell his slaves. To do this, he had to take them to a large city where there was a slave market.

The city was far away, and the slaves must walk the whole distance. A number of bundles were made up for them to carry. Some of these bundles contained the things they would need on the road; some contained clothing; and some contained goods which the master would sell in the city.

"Choose your bundles, boys," said the master. "There is one for each of you."

Aesop at once chose the largest one. The other slaves laughed and said he was foolish. But he threw it upon his shoulders and seemed well satisfied. The next day, the laugh was the other way. For the bundle which he had chosen had contained the food for the whole party. After all had eaten three meals from it, it was very much lighter. And before the end of the journey Aesop had nothing to carry, while the other slaves were groaning under their heavy loads.

"Aesop is a wise fellow," said his master. "The man who buys him must pay a high price."

A very rich man, whose name was Xanthus, [Footnote: Xanthus (*pro* . zan'thus).] came to the slave market to buy a servant. As the slaves stood before him he asked each one to tell what kind of work he could do. All were eager to be bought by Xanthus because they knew he would be a kind master. So each one boasted of his skill in doing some sort of labor. One was a fine gardener; another could take care of horses; a third was a good cook; a fourth could manage a household.

"And what can you do, Aesop?" asked Xanthus.

"Nothing," he answered.

"Nothing? How is that?"

"Because, since these other slaves do everything, there is nothing left for me to perform," said Aesop.

This answer pleased the rich man so well that he bought Aesop at once, and took him to his home on the island of Samos.

In Samos the little slave soon became known for his wisdom and courage. He often amused his master and his master's friends by telling droll fables about birds and beasts that could talk. They saw that all these fables taught some great truth, and they wondered how Aesop could have thought of them.

Many other stories are told of this wonderful slave. His master was so much pleased with him that he gave him his freedom. Many great men were glad to call him their friend, and even kings asked his advice and were amused by his fables.

ONE OF AESOP'S FABLES

An old Cat was in a fair way to kill all the Mice in the barn.

One day the Mice met to talk about the great harm that she was doing them. Each one told of some plan by which to keep out of her way.

"Do as I say," said an old gray Mouse that was thought to be very wise. "Do as I say. Hang a bell to the Cat's neck. Then, when we hear it ring, we shall know that she is coming, and can scamper out of her way." "Good! good!" said all the other Mice; and one ran to get the bell. "Now which of you will hang this bell on the Cat's neck?" said the old gray Mouse.

"Not I! not I!" said all the Mice together. And they scampered away to their holes.

THE DARK DAY

Listen, and I will tell you of the famous dark day in Connecticut. It was in the month of May, more than a hundred years ago.

The sun rose bright and fair, and the morning was without a cloud. The air was very still. There was not a breath of wind to stir the young leaves on the trees.

Then, about the middle of the day, it began to grow dark. The sun was hidden. A black cloud seemed to cover the earth.

The birds flew to their nests. The chickens went to roost. The cows came home from the pasture and stood mooing at the gate. It grew so dark that the people could not see their way along the streets.

Then everybody began to feel frightened. "What is the matter? What is going to happen?" each one asked of another. The children cried. The dogs howled. The women wept, and some of the men prayed.

"The end of the world has come!" cried some; and they ran about in the darkness.

"This is the last great day!" cried others; and they knelt down and waited.

In the old statehouse, the wise men of Connecticut were sitting. They were men who made the laws, and much depended upon their wisdom.

[Illustration]

When the darkness came, they too began to be alarmed. The gloom was terrible.

"It is the day of the Lord." said one.

"No use to make laws," said another, "for they will never be needed."

"I move that we adjourn," said a third.

Then up from his seat rose Abraham Davenport.

His voice was clear and strong, and all knew that he, at least, was not afraid.

"This may be the last great day," he said. "I do not know whether the end of the world has come or not. But I am sure that it is my duty to stand at my post as long as I live. So, let us go on with the work that is before us. Let the candles be lighted."

His words put courage into every heart. The candles were brought in. Then with his strong face aglow in their feeble light, he made a speech in favor of a law to help poor fishermen.

And as he spoke, the other lawmakers listened in silence till the darkness began to fade and the sky grew bright again.

The people of Connecticut still remember Abraham Davenport, because he was a wise judge and a brave lawmaker. The poet Whittier has written a poem about him, which you will like to hear.

THE SURLY GUEST

One day John Randolph, of Roanoke, [Footnote: Ro'a noke.] set out on horseback to ride to a town that was many miles from his home. The road was strange to him, and he traveled very slowly.

When night came on he stopped at a pleasant roadside inn and asked for lodging. The innkeeper welcomed him kindly. He had often heard of the great John Randolph, and therefore he did all that he could to entertain him well.

A fine supper was prepared, and the innkeeper himself waited upon his guest. John Randolph ate in silence. The innkeeper spoke of the weather, of the roads, of the crops, of politics. But his surly guest said scarcely a word.

In the morning a good breakfast was served, and then Mr. Randolph made ready to start on his journey. He called for his bill and paid it. His horse was led to the door, and a servant helped him to mount it.

As he was starting away, the friendly innkeeper said, "Which way will you travel, Mr. Randolph?"

Mr. Randolph looked at him in no gentle way, and answered, "Sir!"

"I only asked which way you intend to travel," said the man.

"Oh! I have I paid you my bill?"

"Yes, sir."

"Do I owe you anything more?"

"No, sir."

"Then, I intend to travel the way I wish to go—do you understand?"

He turned his horse and rode away. He had not gone farther than to the end of the innkeeper's field, when to his surprise he found that the road forked. He did not know whether he should take the right–hand fork or the left–hand.

He paused for a while. There was no signboard to help him. He looked back and saw the innkeeper still standing by the door. He called to him:—"My friend, which of these roads shall I travel to go to Lynchburg?"

"Mr. Randolph," answered the innkeeper, "you have paid your bill and don't owe me a cent. Travel the way you wish to go. Good–by!"

As bad luck would have it, Mr. Randolph took the wrong road. He went far out of his way and lost much time, all on account of his surliness.

[Illustration]

III

John Randolph, of Roanoke, lived in Virginia one hundred years ago. He was famous as a lawyer and statesman. He was a member of Congress for many years, and was noted for his odd manners and strong self– will.

THE STORY OF A GREAT STORY

Two hundred years ago there lived in Scotland a young man whose name was Alexander Selkirk. He was quarrelsome and unruly. He was often making trouble among his neighbors.

For this reason many people were glad when he ran away from home and went to sea. "We hope that he will get what he deserves," they said.

He was big and strong and soon became a fine sailor. But he was still headstrong and ill–tempered; and he was often in trouble with the other sailors.

Once his ship was sailing in the great Pacific Ocean, It was four hundred miles from the coast of South America. Then something happened which Selkirk did not like. He became very disagreeable. He quarreled with the other sailors, and even with the captain.

"I would rather live alone on a desert island than be a sailor on this ship," he said.

"Very well," answered the captain. "We shall put you ashore on the first island that we see."

"Do so," said Selkirk. "You cannot please me better."

The very next day they came in sight of a little green island. There were groves of trees near the shore, and high hills beyond them.

"What is the name of this island?" asked Selkirk.

"Juan Fernandez," [Footnote: Juan Fernandez (pro. joo'an fer nan'dsz).] said the captain.

[Illustration]

"Set me on shore and leave me there. Give me a few common tools and some food, and I will do well enough," said the sailor.

"It shall be done," answered the captain.

So they filled a small boat with the things that he would need the most—an ax, a hoe, a kettle, and some other things. They also put in some bread and meat and other food, enough for several weeks.

Then four of the sailors rowed him to the shore and left him there.

Alexander Selkirk was all alone on the island. He began to see how foolish he had been; he thought how terrible it would be to live there without one friend, without one person to whom he could speak.

He called loudly to the sailors and to the captain. "Oh, do not leave me here. Take me back, and I will give you no more trouble."

But they would not listen to him. The ship sailed away and was soon lost to sight.

Then Selkirk set to work to make the best of things. He built him a little hut for shelter at night and in stormy weather. He planted a small garden. There were pigs and goats on the island, and plenty of fish could be caught from the shore. So there was always plenty of food. Sometimes Selkirk saw ships sailing in the distance. He tried to make signals to them; he called as loudly as he could; but he was neither seen nor heard, and the ships came no nearer.

"If I ever have the good fortune to escape from this island," he said, "I will be kind and obliging to every one. I will try to make friends instead of enemies."

For four years and four months he lived alone on the island. Then, to his great joy, a ship came near and anchored in the little harbor.

He made himself known, and the captain willingly agreed to carry him back to his own country. When he reached Scotland everybody was eager to hear him tell of his adventures, and he soon found himself famous.

In England there was then living a man whose name was Daniel Defoe. [Footnote: De foe'.] He was a writer of books. He had written many stories which people at that time liked to read.

When Daniel Defoe heard how Selkirk had lived alone on the island of Juan Fernandez, he said to himself: "Here is something worth telling about. The story of Alexander Selkirk is very pleasing."

So he sat down and wrote a wonderful story, which he called "The Adventures of Robinson Crusoe."

Every boy has heard of Robinson Crusoe. Many boys and indeed many girls have read his story.

When only a child he liked to stand by the river and see the ships sailing past. He wondered where they had come from and where they were going. He talked with some of the sailors. They told him about the strange lands they had visited far over the sea. They told him about the wonderful things they had seen there. He was delighted.

"Oh, I wish I could be a sailor!" he said.

He could not think of anything else. He thought how grand it would be to sail and sail on the wide blue sea. He thought how pleasant it would be to visit strange countries and see strange peoples.

As he grew up, his father wished him to learn a trade.

"No, no, I am going to be a sailor; I am going to see the world" he said. His mother said to him: "A sailor's life is a hard life. There are great storms on the sea. Many ships are wrecked and the sailors are drowned." "I am not afraid" said Robinson Crusoe. "I am going to be a sailor and nothing else."

So, when he was eighteen years old, he ran away from his pleasant home and went to sea.

He soon found that his mother's words were true.

A sailor's life is indeed a hard life. There is no time to play. Every day there is much work to be done. Sometimes there is great danger.

Robinson Crusoe sailed first on one ship and then on another. He visited many lands and saw many wonderful things.

One day there was a great storm. The ship was driven about by the winds; it was wrecked. All the sailors were drowned but Robinson Crusoe.

He swam to an island that was not far away. It was a small island, and there was no one living on it. But there were birds in the woods and some wild goats on the hills.

For a long time Robinson Crusoe was all alone. He had only a dog and some cats to keep him company. Then he tamed a parrot and some goats.

He built a house of some sticks and vines. He sowed grain and baked bread. He made a boat for himself. He did a great many things. He was busy every day.

At last a ship happened to pass that way and Robinson was taken on board. He was glad to go back to England to see his home and his friends once more.

This is the story which Mr. Defoe wrote. Perhaps he would not have thought of it, had he not first heard the true story of Alexander Selkirk.

THE KING AND THE PAGE

Many years ago there was a king of Prussia, whose name was Frederick; and because he was very wise and very brave, people called him Frederick the Great. Like other kings, he lived in a beautiful palace and had many officers and servants to wait upon him.

Among the servants there was a little page whose name was Carl. It was Carl's duty to sit outside of the king's bedroom and be ready to serve him at any time.

One night the king sat up very late, writing letters and sending messages; and the little page was kept busy running on errands until past midnight.

The next morning the king wished to send him on another errand. He rang the little bell which was used to call the page, but no page answered.

"I wonder what can have happened to the boy," he said; and he opened the door and looked out. There, sitting in his chair, was Carl, fast asleep. The poor child was so tired after his night's work that he could not keep awake.

The king was about to waken him roughly, when he saw a piece of paper on the floor beside him. He picked it up and read it.

It was a letter from the page's mother:—

Dearest Carl; You are a good boy to send me all your wages, for now I can pay the rent and buy some warm clothing for your little sister. I thank you for it, and pray that God will bless you. Be faithful to the king and do your duty.

The king went back to the room on tiptoe. He took ten gold pieces from his table and wrapped them in the little letter. Then he went out again, very quietly, and slipped them all into the boy's pocket.

After a while he rang the bell again, very loudly.

Carl awoke with a start, and came quickly to answer the call.

"I think you have been asleep," said the king.

The boy stammered and did not know what to say. He was frightened and ready to cry.

He put his hand in his pocket, and was surprised to find the gold pieces wrapped in his mother's letter. Then his eyes overflowed with tears, and he fell on his knees before the king.

"What is the matter?" asked Frederick.

"Oh, your Majesty!" cried Carl. "Have mercy on me. It is true that I have been asleep, but I know nothing about this money. Some one is trying to ruin me."

"Have courage, my boy," said the king. "I know how you must have been overwearied with long hours of watching. And people say that fortune comes to us in our sleep. You may send the gold pieces to your mother with my compliments; and tell her that the king will take care of both her and you."

THE HUNTED KING

What boy or girl has not heard the story of King Robert Brace and the spider? I will tell you another story of the same brave and famous king. He had fought a battle with his enemies, the English. His little army had been beaten and scattered. Many of his best friends had been killed or captured. The king himself was obliged to hide in the wild woods while his foes hunted for him with hounds.

For many days he wandered through rough and dangerous places. He waded rivers and climbed mountains. Sometimes two or three faithful friends were with him. Sometimes he was alone. Sometimes his enemies were very close upon him.

Late one evening he came to a little farmhouse in a lonely valley. He walked in without knocking. A woman was sitting alone by the fire.

"May a poor traveler find rest and shelter here for the night?" he asked. The woman answered, "All travelers are welcome for the sake of one; and you are welcome"

"Who is that one?" asked the king.

"That is Robert the Bruce," said the woman. "He is the rightful lord of this country. He is now being hunted with hounds, but I hope soon to see him king over all Scotland."

"Since you love him so well," said the king, "I will tell you something. I am Robert the Bruce."

"You!" cried the woman in great surprise. "Are you the Bruce, and are you all alone?"

"My men have been scattered," said the king, "and therefore there is no one with me."

"That is not right," said the brave woman. "I have two sons who are gallant and trusty. They shall go with you and serve you."

So she called her two sons. They were tall and strong young men, and they gladly promised to go with the king and help him.

[Illustration]

The king sat down by the fire, and the woman hurried to get things ready for supper. The two young men got down their bows and arrows, and all were busy making plans for the next day.

Suddenly a great noise was heard outside. They listened. They heard the tramping of horses and the voices of a number of men.

"The English! the English!" said the young men.

"Be brave, and defend your king with your lives," said their mother.

Then some one outside called loudly, "Have you seen King Robert the Bruce pass this way?"

"That is my brother Edward's voice," said the king. "These are friends, not enemies."

The door was thrown open and he saw a hundred brave men, all ready to give him aid. He forgot his hunger; he forgot his weariness. He began to ask about his enemies who had been hunting him.

"I saw two hundred of them in the village below us," said one of his officers. "They are resting there for the night and have no fear of danger from us. If you have a mind to make haste, we may surprise them."

"Then let us mount and ride," said the king.

The next minute they were off. They rushed suddenly into the village. They routed the king's enemies and scattered them.

And Robert the Bruce was never again obliged to hide in the woods or to run from savage hounds. Soon he became the real king and ruler of all Scotland,

"TRY, TRY AGAIN!"

There was once a famous ruler of Tartary whose name was Tamerlane. Like Alexander the Great, he wished to become the master of the whole world. So he raised a great army and made war against other countries. He conquered many kings and burned many cities.

But at last his army was beaten; his men were scattered; and Tamerlane fled alone from the field of battle.

For a long time he wandered in fear from place to place. His foes were looking for him. He was in despair. He was about to lose all hope.

One day he was lying under a tree, thinking of his misfortunes. He had now been a wanderer for twenty days. He could not hold out much longer. Suddenly he saw a small object creeping up the trunk of the tree. He looked more closely and saw that it was an ant. The ant was carrying a grain of wheat as large as itself.

As Tamerlane looked, he saw that there was a hole in the tree only a little way above, and that this was the home of the ant. "You are a brave fellow, Mr. Ant," he said; "but you have a heavy load to carry."

Just as he spoke, the ant lost its footing and fell to the ground. But it still held on to the grain of wheat.

A second time it tried to carry its load up the rough trunk of the tree, and a second time it failed.

Tamerlane watched the brave little insect. It tried three times, four times, a dozen times, twenty times—but always with the same result.

Then it tried the twenty–first time. Slowly, one little step at a time, it crept up across the rough place where it had slipped and fallen so often. The next minute it ran safely into its home, carrying its precious load. "Well done!" said Tamerlane. "You have taught me a lesson. I, too, will try, try again, till I succeed."

And this he did.

Of what other story does this remind you?

WHY HE CARRIED THE TURKEY

In Richmond, Virginia, one Saturday morning, an old man went into the market to buy something. He was dressed plainly, his coat was worn, and his hat was dingy. On his arm he carried a small basket.

"I wish to get a fowl for to–morrow's dinner," he said.

The market man showed him a fat turkey, plump and white and ready for roasting.

"Ah! that is just what I want," said the old man. "My wife will be delighted with it."

He asked the price and paid for it. The market man wrapped a paper round it and put it in the basket.

Just then a young man stepped up. "I will take one of those turkeys," he said. He was dressed in fine style and carried a small cane.

"Shall I wrap it up for you?" asked the market man.

"Yes, here is your money," answered the young gentleman; "and send it to my house at once."

"I cannot do that," said the market man. "My errand boy is sick to– day, and there is no one else to send. Besides, it is not our custom to deliver goods."

"Then how am I to get it home?" asked the young gentleman.

"I suppose you will have to carry it yourself," said the market man. "It is not heavy."

"Carry it myself! Who do you think I am? Fancy me carrying a turkey along the street!" said the young gentleman; and he began to grow very angry. The old man who had bought the first turkey was standing quite near. He had heard all that was said.

"Excuse me, sir," he said; "but may I ask where you live?"

"I live at Number 39, Blank Street," answered the young gentleman; "and my name is Johnson."

"Well, that is lucky," said the old man, smiling. "I happen to be going that way, and I will carry your turkey, if you will allow me."

"Oh, certainly!" said Mr. Johnson. "Here it is. You may follow me."

When they reached Mr. Johnson's house, the old man politely handed him the turkey and turned to go.

"Here, my friend, what shall I pay you?" said the young gentleman.

"Oh, nothing, sir, nothing," answered the old man. "It was no trouble to me, and you are welcome."

He bowed and went on. Young Mr. Johnson looked after him and wondered. Then he turned and walked briskly back to the market.

"Who is that polite old gentleman who carried my turkey for me?" he asked of the market man.

"That is John Marshall, Chief Justice of the United States. He is one of the greatest men in our country," was the answer.

The young gentleman was surprised and ashamed. "Why did he offer to carry my turkey?" he asked.

"He wished to teach you a lesson," answered the market man.

"What sort of lesson?" "He wished to teach you that no man should feel himself too fine to carry his own packages."

"Oh, no!" said another man who had seen and heard it all. "Judge Marshall carried the turkey simply because he wished to be kind and obliging. That is his way."

THE PADDLE–WHEEL BOAT

More than a hundred years ago, two boys were fishing in a small river. They sat in a heavy flat–bottomed boat, each holding a long, crooked rod in his hands and eagerly waiting for "a bite."

When they wanted to move the boat from one place to another they had to pole it; that is, they pushed against a long pole, the lower end of which reached the bottom of the stream.

"This is slow work, Robert," said the older of the boys as they were poling up the river to a new fishing place. "The old boat creeps over the water no faster than a snail."

"Yes, Christopher; and it is hard work, too," answered Robert. "I think there ought to be some better way of moving a boat."

"Yes, there is a better way, and that is by rowing," said Christopher. "But we have no oars."

"Well, I can make some oars," said Robert; "but I think there ought to be still another and a better way. I am going to find such a way if I can." The next day Robert's aunt heard a great pounding and sawing in her woodshed. The two boys were there, busily working with hammer and saw. "What are you making, Robert?" she asked.

"Oh, I have a plan for making a boat move without poling it or rowing it," he answered.

His aunt laughed and said, "Well, I hope that you will succeed."

After a great deal of tinkering and trying, they did succeed in making two paddle wheels. They were very rough and crude, but strong and serviceable. They fastened each of these wheels to the end of an iron rod which they passed through the boat from side to side. The rod was bent in the middle so that it could be turned as with a crank. When the work was finished, the old fishing boat looked rather odd, with a paddle wheel on each side which dipped just a few inches into the water. The boys lost no time in trying it.

[Illustration]

"She goes ahead all right," said Christopher, "but how shall we guide her?"

"Oh, I have thought of that," said Robert. He took something like an oarlock from his pocket and fastened it to the stern of the boat; then with a paddle which worked in this oarlock one of the boys could guide the boat while the other turned the paddle wheels.

"It is better than poling the boat," said Christopher.

"It is better than rowing, too," said Robert. "See how fast she goes!"

That night when Christopher went home he had a wonderful story to tell. "Bob Fulton planned the whole thing," he said, "and I helped him make the paddles and put them on the boat."

"I wonder why we didn't think of something like that long ago," said his father. "Almost anybody could rig up an old boat like that."

"Yes, I wonder, too," said Christopher. "It looks easy enough, now that Bob has shown how it is done."

When Robert Fulton became a man, he did not forget his experiment with the old fishing boat. He kept on, planning and thinking and working, until at last he succeeded in making a boat with paddle wheels that could be run by steam.

He is now remembered and honored as the inventor of the steamboat. He became famous because he was always thinking and studying and working.

THE CALIPH AND THE GARDENER

There was once a caliph of Cordova whose name was Al Mansour. One day a strange merchant came to him with some diamonds and pearls which he had brought from beyond the sea. The caliph was so well pleased with these jewels that he bought them and paid the merchant a large sum of money. The merchant put the gold in a bag of purple silk which he tied to his belt underneath his long cloak. Then he set out on foot to walk to another city.

It was midsummer, and the day was very hot. As the merchant was walking along, he came to a river that flowed gently between green and shady banks.

He was hot and covered with dust. No one was near. Very few people ever came that way. Why should he not cool himself in the refreshing water? He took off his clothes and laid them on the bank. He put the bag of money on top of them and then leaped into the water. How cool and delicious it was!

Suddenly he heard a rustling noise behind him. He turned quickly and saw an eagle rising into the air with his moneybag in its claws. No doubt the bird had mistaken the purple silk for something good to eat.

The merchant shouted. He jumped out of the water and shouted again. But it was no use. The great bird was high in the air and flying towards the far-off mountains with all his money.

The poor man could do nothing but dress himself and go sorrowing on his way.

A year passed by and then the merchant appeared once more before Al Mansour. "O Caliph," he said, "here are a few jewels which I had reserved as a present for my wife. But I have met with such bad luck that I am forced to sell them. I pray that you will look at them and take them at your own price."

Al Mansour noticed that the merchant was very sad and downcast. "Why, what has happened to you?" he asked. "Have you been sick?"

Then the merchant told him how the eagle had flown away with his money.

"Why didn't you come to us before?" he asked. "We might have done something to help you. Toward what place was the eagle flying when you last saw it?"

"It was flying toward the Black Mountains," answered the merchant.

The next morning the caliph called ten of his officers before him. "Ride at once to the Black Mountains," he said. "Find all the old men that live on the mountains or in the flat country around, and command them to appear before me one week from to-day."

The officers did as they were bidden. On the day appointed, forty gray-bearded, honest old men stood before the caliph. All were asked the same question. "Do you know of any person who was once poor but who has lately and suddenly become well-to-do?"

Most of the old men answered that they did not know of any such person. A few said that there was one man in their neighborhood who seemed to have had some sort of good luck.

This man was a gardener. A year ago he was so poor that he had scarcely clothes for his back. His children were crying for food. But lately everything had changed for him. Both he and his family dressed well; they had plenty to eat; he had even bought a horse to help him carry his produce to market.

The caliph at once gave orders for the gardener to be brought before him the next day. He also ordered that the merchant should come at the same time.

Before noon the next day the gardener was admitted to the palace. As soon as he entered the hall the caliph went to meet him. "Good friend," he said, "if you should find something that we have lost, what would you do with it?"

[Illustration]

The gardener put his hand under his cloak and drew out the very bag that the merchant had lost.

"Here it is, my lord," he said.

At sight of his lost treasure, the merchant began to dance and shout for joy.

"Tell us," said Al Mansour to the gardener, "tell us how you came to find that bag."

The gardener answered: "A year ago, as I was spading in my garden, I saw something fall at the foot of a palm tree. I ran to pick it up and was surprised to find that it was a bag full of bright gold pieces. I said to myself, 'This money must belong to our master, Al Mansour. Some large bird has stolen it from his palace.'"

"Well, then," said the caliph, "why did you not return it to us at once?" "It was this way," said the gardener: "I looked at the gold pieces, and then thought of my own great necessities. My wife and children were suffering from the want of food and clothing. I had no shoes for my feet, no coat for my back. So I said to myself, 'My lord Al Mansour is famous for his kindness to the poor. He will not care.' So I took ten gold pieces from the many that were in the bag.

"I meant only to borrow them. And I put the bag in a safe place, saying that as soon as I could replace the ten pieces, I would return all to my lord Al Mansour. With much hard labor and careful management I have saved only five little silver pieces. But, as I came to your palace this morning, I kept saying to myself, 'When our lord Al Mansour learns just how it was that I borrowed the gold, I have no doubt that in his kindness of heart he will forgive me the debt.'"

Great was the caliph's surprise when he heard the poor man's story. He took the bag of money and handed it to the merchant. "Take the bag and count the money that is in it," he said. "If anything is lacking, I will pay it to you."

The merchant did as he was told. "There is nothing lacking," he said, "but the ten pieces he has told you about; and I will give him these as a reward."

"No," said Al Mansour, "it is for me to reward the man as he deserves."

Saying this, he ordered that ten gold pieces be given to the merchant in place of those that were lacking. Then he rewarded the gardener with ten more pieces for his honesty.

"Your debt is paid. Think no more about it," he said.

THE COWHERD WHO BECAME A POET

I

In England there was once a famous abbey, called Whitby. It was so close to the sea that those who lived in it could hear the waves forever beating against the shore. The land around it was rugged, with only a few fields in the midst of a vast forest.

Fifty Famous People

In those far−off days, an abbey was half church, half castle. It was a place where good people, and timid, helpless people could find shelter in time of war. There they might live in peace and safety while all the country round was overrun by rude and barbarous men.

One cold night in winter the serving men of the abbey were gathered in the great kitchen. They were sitting around the fire and trying to keep themselves warm.

Out of doors the wind was blowing. The men heard it as it whistled through the trees and rattled the doors of the abbey. They drew up closer to the fire and felt thankful that they were safe from the raging storm. "Who will sing us a song?" said the master woodman as he threw a fresh log upon the fire.

"Yes, a song! a song!" shouted some of the others. "Let us have a good old song that will help to keep us warm."

"We can all be minstrels to−night," said the chief cook. "Suppose we each sing a song in turn. What say you?"

"Agreed! agreed!" cried the others. "And the cook shall begin."

The woodman stirred the fire until the flames leaped high and the sparks flew out of the roof hole. Then the chief cook began his song. He sang of war, and of bold rough deeds, and of love and sorrow.

After him the other men were called, one by one; and each in turn sang his favorite song. The woodman sang of the wild forest; the plowman sang of the fields; the shepherd sang of his sheep; and those who listened forgot about the storm and the cold weather.

But in the corner, almost hidden from his fellows, one poor man was sitting who did not enjoy the singing. It was Caedmon, the cowherd. "What shall I do when it comes my turn?" he said to himself. "I do not know any song. My voice is harsh and I cannot sing."

So he sat there trembling and afraid; for he was a timid, bashful man and did not like to be noticed.

At last, just as the blacksmith was in the midst of a stirring song, he rose quietly and went out into the darkness. He went across the narrow yard to the sheds where the cattle were kept in stormy weather.

"The gentle cows will not ask a song of me," said the poor man. He soon found a warm corner, and there he lay down, covering himself with the straw.

Inside of the great kitchen, beside the fire, the men were shouting and laughing; for the blacksmith had finished his song, and it was very pleasing.

"Who is next?" asked the woodman.

"Caedmon, the keeper of the cows," answered the chief cook.

"Yes, Caedmon! Caedmon!" all shouted together. "A song from Caedmon!" But when they looked, they saw that his seat was vacant.

"The poor, timid fellow!" said the blacksmith. "He was afraid and has slipped away from us."

II

In his safe, warm place in the straw, Caedmon soon fell asleep. All around him were the cows of the abbey, some chewing their cuds, and others like their master quietly sleeping. The singing in the kitchen was ended, the fire had burned low, and each man had gone to his place.

Then Caedmon had a strange dream. He thought that a wonderful light was shining around him. His eyes were dazzled by it. He rubbed them with his hands, and when they were quite open he thought that he saw a beautiful face looking down upon him, and that a gentle voice said,—

"Caedmon, sing for me."

At first he was so bewildered that he could not answer. Then he heard the voice again.

"Caedmon, sing something."

"Oh, I cannot sing," answered the poor man." I do not know any song; and my voice is harsh and unpleasant. It was for this reason that I left my fellows in the abbey kitchen and came here to be alone."

"But you *must* sing," said the voice. "You *must* sing."

"What shall I sing?" he asked.

"Sing of the creation," was the answer.

Then Caedmon, with only the cows as his hearers, opened his mouth and began to sing. He sang of the beginning of things; how the world was made; how the sun and moon came into being; how the land rose from the water; how the birds and the beasts were given life.

[Illustration: Caedmon signing in the cow byre]

All through the night he sat among the abbey cows, and sang his wonderful song. When the stable boys and shepherds came out in the morning, they heard him singing; and they were so amazed that they stood still in the drifted snow and listened with open mouths.

At length, others of the servants heard him, and were entranced by his wonderful song. And one ran quickly and told the good abbess, or mistress of the abbey, what strange thing had happened.

"Bring the cowherd hither, that I and those who are with me may hear him," said she.

So Caedmon was led into the great hall of the abbey. And all of the sweet-faced sisters and other women of the place listened while he sang again the wonderful song of the creation.

"Surely," said the abbess, "this is a poem, most sweet, most true, most beautiful. It must be written down so that people in other places and in other times may hear it read and sung."

So she called her clerk, who was a scholar, and bade him write the song, word for word, as it came from Caedmon's lips. And this he did.

Such was the way in which the first true English poem was written. And Caedmon, the poor cowherd of the abbey, was the first great poet of England.

THE LOVER OF MEN

In the Far East there was once a prince whose name was Gautama. He lived in a splendid palace where there was everything that could give delight. It was the wish of his father and mother that every day of his life should be a day of perfect happiness.

So this prince grew up to be a young man, tall and fair and graceful. He had never gone beyond the beautiful gardens that surrounded his father's palace. He had never seen nor heard of sorrow or sickness or poverty. Everything that was evil or disagreeable had been carefully kept out of his sight. He knew only of those things that give joy and health and peace.

But one day after he had become a man, he said: "Tell me about the great world which, you say, lies outside of these palace walls. It must be a beautiful and happy place; and I wish to know all about it." "Yes, it is a beautiful place," was the answer. "In it there are numberless trees and flowers and rivers and waterfalls, and other things to make the heart glad."

"Then to-morrow I will go out and see some of those things," he said.

His parents and friends begged him not to go. They told him that there were beautiful things at home—why go away to see other things less beautiful? But when they saw that his mind was set on going, they said no more.

The next morning, Gautama sat in his carriage and rode out from the palace into one of the streets of the city. He looked with wonder at the houses on either side, and at the faces of the children who stood in the doorways as he passed. At first he did not see anything that disturbed him; for word had gone before him to remove from sight everything that might be displeasing or painful.

Soon the carriage turned into another street—a street less carefully guarded. Here there were no children at the doors. But suddenly, at a narrow place, they met a very old man, hobbling slowly along over the stony way.

"Who is that man?" asked Gautama, "and why is his face so pinched and his hair so white? Why do his legs tremble under him as he walks, leaning upon a stick? He seems weak, and his eyes are dull. Is he some new kind of man?"

"Sir," answered the coachman, "that is an old man. He has lived more than eighty years. All who reach old age must lose their strength and become like him, feeble and gray."

"Alas!" said the prince. "Is this the condition to which I must come?"

"If you live long enough," was the answer.

"What do you mean by that? Do not all persons live eighty years—yes, many times eighty years?"

The coachman made no answer, but drove onward.

They passed out into the open country and saw the cottages of the poor people. By the door of one of these a sick man was lying upon a couch, helpless and pale.

"Why is that man lying there at this time of day?" asked the prince. "His face is white, and he seems very weak. Is he also an old man?"

"Oh, no! He is sick," answered the coachman. "Poor people are often sick." "What does that mean?" asked the prince. "Why are they sick?"

The coachman explained as well as he was able; and they rode onward.

Soon they saw a company of men toiling by the roadside. Their faces were browned by the sun; their hands were hard and gnarly; their backs were bent by much heavy lifting; their clothing was in tatters.

"Who are those men, and why do their faces look so joyless?" asked the prince. "What are they doing by the roadside?"

"They are poor men, and they are working to improve the king's highway," was the answer.

"Poor men? What does that mean?"

"Most of the people in the world are poor," said the coachman. "Their lives are spent in toiling for the rich. Their joys are few; their sorrows are many."

"And is this the great, beautiful, happy world that I have been told about?" cried the prince. "How weak and foolish I have been to live in idleness and ease while there is so much sadness and trouble around me. Turn the carriage quickly, coachman, and drive home. Henceforth, I will never again seek my own pleasure. I will spend all my life, and give all that I have, to lessen the distress and sorrow with which this world seems filled."

This the prince did. One night he left the beautiful palace which his father had given to him and went out into the world to do good and to help his fellow men. And to this day, millions of people remember and honor the name of Gautama, as that of the great lover of men.

THE CHARCOAL MAN AND THE KING

There once lived in Paris a poor charcoal man whose name was Jacquot. [Footnote: *pro.* zhak ko'] His house was small, with only one room in it; but it was large enough for Jacquot and his wife and their two little boys.

At one end of the room there was a big fireplace, where the mother did the cooking. At the other end were the beds. And in the middle was a rough table with benches around it instead of chairs.

Jacquot's business was to sell charcoal to the rich people in the city. He might be seen every day with a bag of charcoal on his back, carrying it to some of his customers. Sometimes he carried three or four bags to the palace where the little king of France lived with his mother.

One evening he was very late coming home. The table was spread and supper was ready. The children were hungry and could hardly wait for their father to come.

"The supper will get cold," said Charlot,[Footnote: *pro.* shar lo'] the eldest.

"I wonder why he is so late," said his little brother, Blondel.[Footnote: Blon del'.]

"There is to be a great feast at the queen's palace to–night," said the mother." There will be music and dancing, and many fine people will be there. Perhaps your father is waiting to help in the kitchen."

The next minute they heard his voice at the door: "Be quick, boys, and stir the fire. Throw on some chips and make a blaze."

They did so, and as the flames lighted up the room, they saw their father enter with a child in his arms.

"What's the matter?" cried the mother. "Who is that child?"

Then she saw that the child's face was very pale and that he neither opened his eyes nor moved.

"Oh, what has happened? Where did you find him?"

"I'll tell you all about it," answered Jacquot. "But first get a blanket and warm it, quick. That on the children's bed is best."

"What a beautiful child!" said the mother, as she hurried to do his bidding. The two boys, Charlot and Blondel, with wondering eyes watched their father and mother undress the little stranger. His beautiful clothes were soaked with water, and his fine white collar and ruffles were soiled and dripping.

"He must have some dry clothes. Bring me your Sunday suit, Charlot."

"Here it is, mother." said Charlot.

Soon the little stranger was clad in the warm clothes; the dry soft blanket was wrapped around him; and he was laid on the children's bed.

Then, being very comfortable, he began to grow stronger. The color came back to his cheeks. He opened his eyes and looked around at the small, plain room and at the poor people standing near him.

"Where am I? Where am I?" he asked.

"In my house, my little friend," answered Jacquot.

"*My little friend!*" said the child with a sneer.

He looked at the fire on the hearth, and at the rough table and benches. Then he said, "Your house is a very poor place, I think."

"I am sorry if you do not like it," said Jacquot. "But if I had not helped you, you would have been in a worse place."

"How did these clothes come on me?" cried the child. "They are not mine. You have stolen my clothes and have given me these ugly things."

"Stolen!" said the charcoal man, angrily. "What do you mean, you ungrateful little rascal?"

"Hush, Jacquot," said his wife, kindly. "He doesn't know what he says. Wait till he rests a while, and then he'll be in a better humor."

The child was indeed very tired. His eyes closed and he was soon fast asleep.

"Now tell us, father," whispered Charlot, "where did you find him?"

The charcoal man sat down by the fire. The two boys stood at his knees, and his wife sat at his side.

"I will tell you," he said. "I had carried some charcoal to the queen's kitchen and was just starting home. I took the shortest way through the little park behind the palace. You know where the fountain is?"

"Yes, yes!" said Blondel. "It is quite near the park gate."

"Well, as I was hurrying along, I heard a great splash, as though something had fallen into the pool by the fountain. I looked and saw this little fellow struggling in the water. I ran and pulled him out. He was almost drowned."

"Did he say anything, father?" asked Charlot.

"Oh, no! He was senseless; but I knew he wasn't drowned. I thought of the big fire in the queen's kitchen, and knew that the cook would never allow a half–drowned child to be carried into that fine place. Then I thought of our own warm little house, and how snug we could make him until he came to his senses again. So I took him in my arms and ran home as fast as I could."

"The poor, dear child!" said Mrs. Jacquot. "I wonder who he is."

"He shall be our little brother," said Blondel; and both the boys clapped their hands very softly.

In a little while the child awoke. He seemed to feel quite well and strong. He sat up in the bed and looked around.

"You want your mother, don't you?" said Mrs. Jacquot. "She must be very uneasy about you. Tell us who she is, and we will carry you to her." "There is no hurry about that," said the child.

"But they will be looking for you."

"So much the better, let them look. My mother will not be worried. She has other things to do, and no time to attend to me."

"What! Your own mother, and no time to attend to her child?"

"Yes, madam. But she has servants to attend to me." "Servants! Yes, I think so," said Jacquot. "They let you fall into the water, and you would have been drowned, if it hadn't been for me. But come, children, let us have our supper."

They sat down at the table. The mother gave each a tin plate and a wooden spoon, and then helped them all to boiled beans. The father cut slices from a loaf of brown bread.

The little stranger came and sat with them. But he would not eat anything.

"You must tell us who your mother is," said Mrs. Jacquot. "We must let her know that you are safe."

"Of course she will be glad to know that," said the boy; "but she has no time to bother about me to–night."

"Is she like our mother?" asked Chariot.

"She is handsomer."

"But ours is better. She is always doing something for us," said Blondel.

"Mine gives me fine clothes and plenty of money to spend," said the stranger.

73

"Ours gives us kisses," said Charlot.

"Ha! that's nothing. Mine makes the servants wait on me and do as I tell them."

"But our dear mother waits on us herself."

The charcoal man and his wife listened to this little dispute, and said nothing. They were just rising from the table when they heard a great noise in the street. Then there was a knock at the door.

Before Mrs. Jacquot could open it, some one called out, "Is this the house of Jacquot, the charcoal man?"

"That is my tutor," whispered the little stranger. "He has come after me." Then he slipped quickly under the table and hid himself. "Don't tell him I am here," he said softly.

In a few minutes the room was filled with gentlemen. They were all dressed very finely, and some of them carried swords.

A tall man who wore a long red cloak seemed to be the leader of the company. He said to a soldier who stood at the door, "Tell your story again."

"Well," said the soldier, "about two hours ago I was on guard at the gate of the queen's park. This charcoal man, whom I know very well, ran past me with a child in his arms. I did not—"

"That will do, sir," said the man in red. "Now, you charcoal man, where is that child?"

"Here!" cried the child himself, darting out from his hiding place.

[Illustration]

"O your Majesty!" said the man in red. "All your court has been looking for you for the past two hours."

"I am glad to hear it, Cardinal Mazarin," [Footnote: Maz a reen'.] said the boy.

"Your mother is very anxious."

"I am sorry if I have given her trouble. But really, I fell into the pool at the fountain, and this kind man brought me here to get me dry."

"Indeed!" said the cardinal. "But I hope you are now ready to come home with us."

"I shall go when I please."

"Your mother—"

"Oh, yes, I know she is anxious, and I will go. But first I must thank these poor people."

"Please do so, your Majesty."

The boy turned toward the charcoal man and said:—"My friend, I am the king of France. My name is Louis the Fourteenth. I thank you for what you have done for me. You shall have money to buy a larger house and to send your boys to school. Here is my hand to kiss." Then he turned to the cardinal and said, "Now, I am ready. Let us go."

Not dressed in that way?" said the cardinal. He had just noticed that the king was wearing poor Charlot's Sunday suit instead of his own.

"Why not?" answered the little king.

"Think what your mother would say if she saw you in the clothes of a poor man's son." said the cardinal. "Think of what all the fine ladies would say."

"Let them say what they please, I am not going to change my clothes."

As the little king went out, he turned at the door and called to Charlot. "Come to the palace to—morrow," he said, "and you shall have your clothes. You may bring mine with you."

Louis the Fourteenth became king of France when he was only five years old. He was called "the Fourteenth" because there had been thirteen other kings before him who bore the name of Louis. In history he is often called the Grand Monarch.

WHICH WAS THE KING?

One day King Henry the Fourth of France was hunting in a large forest. Towards evening he told his men to ride home by the main road while he went by another way that was somewhat longer.

As he came out of the forest he saw a little boy by the roadside, who seemed to be watching for some one.

"Well, my boy," said the king, "are you looking for your father?"

"No, sir," answered the boy. "I am looking for the king. They say he is hunting in the woods, and perhaps will ride out this way. So I'm waiting to see him."

"Oh, if that is what you wish," said King Henry, "get up behind me on the horse and I'll take you to the place where you will see him."

The boy got up at once, and sat behind the king. The horse cantered briskly along, and king and boy were soon quite well acquainted.

"They say that King Henry always has a number of men with him," said the boy; "how shall I know which is he?"

"Oh, that will be easy enough," was the answer. "All the other men will take off their hats, but the king will keep his on."

"Do you mean that the one with his hat on will be the king?"

"Certainly."

Soon they came into the main road where a number of the king's men were waiting. All the men seemed amused when they saw the boy, and as they rode up, they greeted the king by taking off their hats.

"Well, my boy," said King Henry, "which do you think is the king?"

"I don't know," answered the boy; "but it must be either you or I, for we both have our hats on."

THE GOLDEN TRIPOD

I

One morning, long ago, a merchant of Miletus [Footnote: Mile'tus.] was walking along the seashore. Some fishermen were pulling in a large net, and he stopped to watch them.

"My good men," he said, "how many fish do you expect to draw in this time?"

"We cannot tell," they answered. "We never count our fish before they are caught."

The net seemed heavy. There was certainly something in it. The merchant felt sure that the fishermen were having a good haul.

"How much will you take for the fish that you are drawing in?" he asked.

"How much will you give?" said the fishermen.

"Well, I will give three pieces of silver for all that are in the net," answered the merchant.

[Illustration]

The fishermen talked in low tones with one another for a little while, and then one said, "It's a bargain. Be they many or few, you may have all for three pieces of silver."

In a few minutes the big net was pulled up out of the water. There was not a fish in it. But it held a beautiful golden tripod that was worth more than a thousand fishes.

76

The merchant was delighted. "Here is your money," he said. "Give me the tripod."

"No, indeed," said the fishermen. "You were to have all the fish that happened to be in the net and nothing else. We didn't sell you the tripod."

They began to quarrel. They talked and wrangled a long time and could not agree. Then one of the fishermen said, "Let us ask the governor about it and do as he shall bid us."

"Yes, let us ask the governor," said the merchant. "Let him decide the matter for us."

So they carried the tripod to the governor, and each told his story.

The governor listened, but could not make up his mind as to who was right. "This is a very important question," he said. "We must send to Delphi [Footnote: Delphi (*pro.* del'fi).] and ask the oracle whether the tripod shall be given to the fishermen or to the merchant. Leave the tripod in my care until we get an answer."

Now the oracle at Delphi was supposed to be very wise. People from all parts of the world sent to it, to tell it their troubles and get its advice.

So the governor sent a messenger to Delphi to ask the oracle what should be done with the tripod. The merchant and the fishermen waited impatiently till the answer came. And this is what the oracle said:—

"Give not the merchant nor the fishermen the prize; But give it to that one who is wisest of the wise."

The governor was much pleased with this answer.

"The prize shall go to the man who deserves it most," he said. "There is our neighbor, Thales,[Footnote: Thales (pro. tha'leez).] whom everybody knows and loves. He is famous all over the world. Men come from every country to see him and learn from him. We will give the prize to him."

So, with his own hands he carried the golden tripod to the little house where Thales lived. He knocked at the door and the wise man himself opened it.

Then the governor told him how the tripod had been found, and how the oracle had said that it must be given to the wisest of the wise.

"And so I have brought the prize to you, friend Thales."

"To me!" said the astonished Thales. "Why, there are many men who are wiser than I. There is my friend Bias [Footnote: Bi'as] of Priene. [Footnote: Prie'ne] He excels all other men. Send the beautiful gift to him."

So the governor called two of his trusted officers and told them to carry the tripod to Priene and offer it to Bias.

"Tell the wise man why you bring it, and repeat to him the words of the oracle."

II

Now all the world had heard of the wisdom of Bias. He taught that men ought to be kind even to their enemies. He taught, also, that a friend is the greatest blessing that any one can have.

He was a poor man and had no wish to be rich. "It is better to be wise than wealthy," he said.

When the governor's messengers came to Priene with the tripod, they found Bias at work in his garden. They told him their errand and showed him the beautiful prize.

He would not take it.

"The oracle did not intend that I should have it," he said. "I am not the wisest of the wise."

"But what shall we do with it?" said the messengers. "Where shall we find the wisest man?"

"In Mitylene," [Footnote: Mit y l e'ne.] answered Bias, "there is a very great man named Pittacus. [Footnote: Pit'ta ous.] He might now be the king of his country, but he prefers to give all of his time to the study of wisdom. He is the man whom the oracle meant."

III

The name of Pittacus was known all over the world. He was a brave soldier and a wise teacher. The people of his country had made him their king; but as soon as he had made good laws for them he gave up his crown.

One of his mottoes was this: "Whatever you do, do it well."

The messengers found him in his house talking to his friends and teaching them wisdom. He looked at the tripod. "How beautiful it is!" he said.

Then the messengers told him how it had been taken from the sea, and they repeated the words of the oracle:—

"Give not the merchant nor the fishermen the prize; But give it to that one who is wisest of the wise."

"It is well," said he, "that neither a merchant nor a fisherman shall have it; for such men think only of their business and care really nothing for beauty."

"We agree with you," said the messengers; "and we present the prize to you because you are the wisest of the wise."

"You are mistaken," answered Pittacus. "I should be delighted to own so beautiful a piece of workmanship, but I know I am not worthy."

"Then to whom shall we take it?" asked the messengers.

"Take it to Cleobulus, [Footnote: Cle o bu'lus.] King of Rhodes, [Footnote: Rhodes (*pro.* rodes).]" answered the wise man. "He is the handsomest and strongest of men, and I believe he is the wisest also."

IV

The messengers went on until they came at last to the island of Rhodes. There everybody was talking about King Cleobulus and his wonderful wisdom. He had studied in all the great schools of the world, and there was nothing that he did not know.

"Educate the children," he said; and for that reason his name is remembered to this day.

When the messengers showed him the tripod, he said, "That is indeed a beautiful piece of work. Will you sell it? What is the price?"

They told him that it was not for sale, but that it was to be given to the wisest of the wise.

"Well, you will not find that man in Rhodes," said he. "He lives in Corinth, [Footnote: Cor'inth.] and his name is Periander. [Footnote: Per i an'der.] Carry the precious gift to him."

V

Everybody had heard of Periander, king of Corinth. Some had heard of his great learning, and others had heard of his selfishness and cruelty.

Strangers admired him for his wisdom. His own people despised him for his wickedness.

When he heard that some men had come to Corinth with a very costly golden tripod, he had them brought before him.

"I have heard all about that tripod," he said, "and I know why you are carrying it from one place to another. Do you expect to find any man in Corinth who deserves so rich a gift?"

"We hope that you are the man," said the messengers.

"Ha! ha I" laughed Periander. "Do I look like the wisest of the wise? No, indeed. But in Lacedaemon [Footnote: Lacedaemon (*pro.* las e de'mon).] there is a good and noble man named Chilon.[Footnote: Chilon (*pro.* ki'lon).] He loves his country, he loves his fellow men, he loves learning. To my mind he deserves the golden prize. I bid you carry it to him.”

VI

The messengers were surprised. They had never heard of Chilon, for his name was hardly known outside of his own country. But when they came into Lacedaemon, they heard his praises on every side.

They learned that Chilon was a very quiet man, that he never spoke about himself, and that he spent all his time in trying to make his country great and strong and happy.

Chilon was so busy that the messengers had to wait several days before they could see him. At last they were allowed to go before him and state their business.

“We have here a very beautiful tripod,” they said. “The oracle at Delphi has ordered that it shall be given to the wisest of wise men, and for that reason we have brought it to you.”

“You have made a mistake,” said Chilon. “Over in Athens [Footnote: Ath'ens.] there is a very wise man whose name is Solon. [Footnote: So'lon.] He is a poet, a soldier, and a lawmaker. He is my worst enemy, and yet I admire him as the wisest man in the world. It is to him that you should have taken the tripod.”

VII

The messengers made due haste to carry the golden prize to Athens. They had no trouble in finding Solon. He was the chief ruler of that great city.

All the people whom they saw spoke in praise of his wisdom.

When they told him their errand he was silent for a little while; then he said:—

“I have never thought of myself as a wise man, and therefore the prize is not for me. But I know of at least six men who are famous for their wisdom, and one of them must be the wisest of the wise.”

“Who are they?” asked the messengers.

“Their names are Thales, Bias, Pittacus, Cleobulus, Periander, and Chilon,” answered Solon.

“We have offered the prize to each one of them,” said the messengers, “and each one has refused it.”

“Then there is only one other thing to be done,” said Solon. “Carry it to Delphi and leave it there in the Temple of Apollo; for Apollo is the fountain of wisdom, the wisest of the wise.”

And this the messengers did.

The famous men of whom I have told you in this story are commonly called the Seven Wise Men of Greece. They lived more than two thousand years ago, and each one helped to make his country famous.

FIFTY FAMOUS PEOPLE

Who they were, what they were, where they lived,

Aesop	Fabulist	Greece	550—? B.C.
Alexander	King	Macedon	356—323 B.C.
Alfred the Great	King	England	849—901
Al Mansour	Caliph	Spain	939—1002
Al Mansur	Caliph	Persia	712—775
Arion	Musician	Greece	6th Century B.C.
Aristomenes	General	Greece	685—? B.C.
Bruce, Robert	King	Sweden	1274—1329
Burritt, Elihu	Philanthropist	Connecticut	1811—1879
Caedmon	Poet	England	650—720 (?)
Charles XII	King	Sweden	1682—1718
Coriolanus	General	Rome	5th Century B.C.
Cyrus	King	Persia	6th Century B.C.
Davenport, A.	Legislator	Connecticut	1715—1780
Everett, Edward	Statesman	Massachusetts	1794—1865
Franklin, Benj.	Statesman	Pennsylvania	1706—1790
Frederick the Great	King	Prussia	1712—1786
Fulton, Robert	Inventor	New York	1765—1815
Gautama	Prince	India	562—472 B.C.
Giotto, Bondone	Painter	Italy	1276—1337
Haroun al Raschid	Caliph	Bagdad	750—809
Henry IV	King	France	1553—1610
Hogg, James	Poet	Scotland	1770—1835
Jackson, Andrew	President	United States	1767—1835
Jefferson, Thos.	President	United States	1743—1826
Jones, Sir William	Scholar	England	1746—1794
Lafayette	General	France	1757—1834
Lee, Robert E.	General	Virginia	1807—1870
Lincoln, Abraham	President	United States	1809—1865
Longfellow, H. W.	Poet	Massachusetts	1807—1882
Louis XIV	King	France	1638—1715
Mamoun	Caliph	Persia	785—?
Marshall, John	Statesman	Virginia	1755—1835
Otanes	General	Persia	6th Century B.C.
Psammeticus	King	Egypt	7th Century B.C.

Putnam, Israel   General   Connecticut   1718—1790
Randolph, John   Statesman   Virginia   1773—1833
Revere, Paul   Patriot   Massachusetts 1735—1818
Richard III   King   England   1452—1485
St. Francis   Saint   Italy   1182—1226
Selkirk, Alexander Sailor   Scotland   1676—1723
Solomon   King   Jerusalem   10th Century B.C.
Solon   Philosopher Athens   6th Century B.C.
Swift, Jonathan   Author   Ireland   1667—1745
Tamerlane   Conqueror   Tartary   1333—1405
Thales   Philosopher Miletus   6th Century B.C.
Washington, G.   President   United States 1732—1799
Webster, Daniel   Statesman   Massachusetts 1782—1852
West, Benjamin   Painter   Pennsylvania 1738—1820
Zeuxis   Painter   Greece   5th Century B.C.

A few other famous people mentioned in this volume.

Astyages   King   Media   6th Century B.C.
Bias   Philosopher Priene   6th Century B.C.
Chilon   Philosopher Sparta   6th Century B.C.
Cimabue   Painter   Florence   1240—1302
Cleobulus   King   Rhodes   6th Century B.C.
Defoe, Daniel Author   England   1661—1731
Mazarin   Cardinal   France   1602—1661
Parrhasius   Painter   Greece   —400 B.C.
Periander   King   Corinth   6th Century B.C.
Pittacus   Philosopher Mitylene   6th Century B.C.
Sheba, The Queen of   10th Century B.C.

CPSIA information can be obtained at www.ICGtesting.com
Printed in the USA
LVOW032200080812

293435LV00007BA/50/P